ELON MUSK

AMERICAN OLIGARCH

OTHER GRAPHIC BOOKS BY DARRYL CUNNINGHAM

Psychiatric Tales

How to Fake a Moon Landing (UK title: *Science Tales*)

The Age of Selfishness (UK title: *Supercrash*)

Graphic Science: Seven Stories of Discovery

Billionaires: The Lives of the Rich and Powerful

Putin: The Rise of a Dictator

ELON MUSK

AMERICAN OLIGARCH

DARRYL
CUNNINGHAM

SEVEN STORIES PRESS
new york • oakland

Originally published in French under the following title:
Elon Musk, Enquête sur un nouveau maître du monde by Darryl Cunningham

Seven Stories Press
140 Watts Street
New York, NY 10013
www.sevenstories.com

Library of Congress Cataloging-in-Publication Data is on file.

Printed in Singapore.

9 8 7 6 5 4 3 2 1

CONTENTS

EARLY YEARS

ELON REEVE MUSK WAS BORN JUNE 28, 1971.
PRETORIA, SOUTH AFRICA.
SOUTH AFRICA AT THAT TIME WAS A WHITE NATIONALIST REGIME THAT PRACTICED APARTHEID OR "APARTNESS" IN THE LANGUAGE OF AFRIKAANS.
A SYSTEM OF LEGISLATION THAT UPHELD SEGREGATIONIST POLICIES AGAINST NON-WHITE CITIZENS.
THE SYSTEM OF APARTHEID RACIALLY STRATIFIED SOCIETY, GRANTING WHITE CITIZENS THE HIGHEST STATUS, FOLLOWED BY INDIANS AND BLACK PEOPLE. BLACK AFRICANS WERE CONSIDERED THE LOWEST.
APARTHEID DENIED NON-WHITE SOUTH AFRICANS BASIC HUMAN RIGHTS. NON-WHITES COULD NOT VOTE. THEY WERE FORCED TO LIVE IN SEPARATE AREAS FROM WHITES AND USE SEPARATE PUBLIC FACILITIES.
WHITES ONLY

RESISTANCE TO APARTHEID WAS BRUTALLY REPRESSED.
TO LIVE IN ONE OF THE SEGREGATED WHITE COMMUNITIES WAS TO BE CONSTANTLY EXPOSED TO ANTI-BLACK GOVERNMENT PROPAGANDA.
THESE SO-CALLED FREEDOM FIGHTERS ARE JUST TERRORISTS.
THERE WAS AN ATTEMPT TO DISASSOCIATE THE WHITE POPULATION FROM THE ATROCITIES THAT POLITICAL LEADERS INFLICTED ON THE BLACK MAJORITY.
WE JUST WANT TO PROTECT OUR WAY OF LIFE.
NEWSPAPERS WOULD HAVE SECTIONS BLACKED OUT. EVENING NEWS BULLETINS WOULD END WITH THE NATIONAL ANTHEM AND SCROLLING THE NAMES OF WHITE YOUNG MEN WHO'D DIED FIGHTING TO PRESERVE THE RACIST REGIME.
THE INTERNATIONAL COMMUNITY SUPPORTS APARTHEID. I'VE NEVER READ ANYTHING TO SAY THEY DON'T.
NEVERTHELESS, AS A CHILD, MUSK WOULD HAVE BEEN CONFRONTED WITH THE EVIDENCE OF INJUSTICE EVERY DAY.
THE DIVISIONAL COUNCIL OF THE CAPE
WHITE AREA
BY ORDER SECRETARY
DIE AFDELINGSRAAD VAN DIE KAAP
BLANKE GEBIED
OP LAS SEKRETARIS
MUSK TURNED FOUR YEARS OLD ONLY DAYS AFTER THE SOWETO UPRISING, WHEN HUNDREDS OF BLACK STUDENTS WERE SHOT DEAD PROTESTING THE WHITE GOVERNMENT.

IT'S NOT POSSIBLE TO DISCUSS ELON MUSK'S BACKGROUND WITHOUT MENTIONING HIS GRANDFATHER, JOSHUA NORMAN HALDEMAN.
BORN IN 1902 IN A LOG CABIN IN MINNESOTA, USA. A PLACE HE DIDN'T REMAIN LONG.
BECAUSE IN 1907, HALDEMAN'S FATHER (JOHN ELON HALDEMAN) UPROOTED HIS FAMILY AND TOOK THEM TO SASKATCHEWAN IN CANADA, AND THEN PROMPTLY DIED.
CANADA
USA
YOUNG JOSHUA NORMAN WAS ADVENTUROUS FROM THE BEGINNING. HE TOOK UP BOXING, WRESTLING, AND BRONCO HORSEBACK RIDING.
LOOK AT MY ROPING SKILLS.
AS A TEEN HE LEFT FOR IOWA, WHERE HE EARNED A DEGREE AT THE PALMER COLLEGE OF CHIROPRACTIC.
THEN HE RETURNED TO SASKATCHEWAN, WHERE HE PRACTICED AS A CHIROPRACTOR BEFORE TRYING HIS HAND AS A FARMER.

THE FARM WAS LOST DURING THE 1930S DEPRESSION WHEN HE COULD NOT KEEP UP WITH BANK LOANS.
THIS 5000 ACRE FARM Will Be Sold at PUBLIC AUCTION
HALDEMAN THEN BEGAN TO WORK AS A CHIROPRACTOR, BUILDING UP A BOOMING PRACTICE. HE MARRIED A WOMAN CALLED EVE PETERS, WITH WHOM HE HAD A SON, BUT THE MARRIAGE DIDN'T LAST.
HIS SECOND WIFE WAS WINNIFRED JOSEPHINE FLETCHER, A DANCE INSTRUCTOR. THE COUPLE HAD FIVE CHILDREN: TWO SONS AND THREE GIRLS, TWO OF WHOM WERE TWINS (KAYE AND MAYE).
HALDEMAN WAS INVOLVED IN THE FOUNDING OF THE DOMINION COUNCIL OF CANADIAN CHIROPRACTORS (LATER THE CANADIAN CHIROPRACTIC ASSOCIATION).
WHILE HE WAS WITH THIS ORGANIZATION HE HELPED PLAN THE FOUNDING OF THE COUNTRY'S FIRST CHIROPRACTIC COLLEGE, WHICH OPENED IN TORONTO IN 1945.
HIS POLITICAL VIEWS WERE UNORTHODOX. BETWEEN 1936 AND 1941, HE BECAME A MEMBER OF THE TECHNOCRACY PARTY, EVENTUALLY BECOMING LEADER OF THE CANADIAN BRANCH.

THE NOW ALMOST-FORGOTTEN TECHNOCRACY MOVEMENT WAS POPULAR IN THE US AND CANADA FOR A BRIEF PERIOD IN THE 1930S AND EARLY 1940S.
OFFICIAL SYMBOL OF THE TECHNOCRACY MOVEMENT.
IT PROPOSED A FORM OF GOVERNMENT IN WHICH DECISION-MAKERS WERE SELECTED BASED ON SPECIALIZED KNOWLEDGE RATHER THAN POLITICAL PARTY, PARLIAMENTARY SKILLS, OR POPULARITY.
TECHNOCRACY
INCORPORATED
MEETS EACH MONDAY EVENING
BASEMENT OF PUBLIC LIBRARY
IN OTHER WORDS, SCIENTISTS AND ENGINEERS WOULD TAKE OVER THE GOVERNMENT AND ECONOMY FROM POLITICIANS.
TECHNOCRACY INC.
YES
SCIENCE CAN DISTRIBUTE OUR ABUNDANCE
INVESTIGATE TECHNOCRACY NOW
IT WAS A SCIENCE-BASED MOVEMENT THAT BY ITS NATURE CLASHED WITH THE IDEALS OF REPRESENTATIVE DEMOCRACY. THERE WAS MORE THAN A WHIFF OF FASCISM ABOUT TECHNOCRACY.
WILL I GET A VOTE IN THIS WONDROUS NEW TECHNO-UTOPIA, OR HAVE ANY SAY AT ALL?
CRITICS OF THE MOVEMENT POINTED OUT THAT TECHNOCRACY WOULD MARGINALIZE THE GENERAL PUBLIC AND CREATE AN ELITE RULING CLASS.
SECTION R.D.11834
THERE WAS A PLAN FOR A NORTH AMERICAN TECHNATE THAT WOULD HAVE TRANSFORMED NORTH AMERICA INTO ONE HUGE TECHNOCRATIC SOCIETY.
THE TECHNATE WOULD HAVE INCLUDED CANADA, MEXICO, CENTRAL AMERICA, AND PART OF SOUTH AMERICA.

DURING THE SECOND WORLD WAR, THE CANADIAN GOVERNMENT TEMPORARILY BANNED THE TECHNOCRACY PARTY DUE TO FEARS OF ITS REVOLUTIONARY. NATURE.
HALDEMAN RESIGNED FROM THE PARTY IN 1941 WHEN ITS CENTRAL OFFICE CHANGED ITS POLICIES FROM OPPOSITION TO COMMUNISM TO "ECONOMIC AND MILITARY COLLABORATION WITH SOVIET RUSSIA" AFTER NAZI GERMANY'S INVASION OF THE USSR.
WHERE YOU GOING?
THIS WAS A POLITICAL POSITION THE SERIOUSLY ANTI-COMMUNIST HALDEMAN COULD NOT STOMACH, EVEN IF IT MEANT HELPING DEFEAT THE NAZIS.
FROM 1941 TO 1943, HE ATTEMPTED TO ESTABLISH HIS OWN POLITICAL PARTY, AND WHEN THAT CAME TO NOTHING, HE JOINED THE SOCIAL CREDIT PARTY OF CANADA.
WELCOME.
THIS WAS A MINOR CANADIAN POLITICAL PARTY THAT PROMOTED IDEAS OF MONETARY REFORM.
SO YOU WANT TO DISTRIBUTE MONEY TO INCREASE SPENDING AND STIMULATE ECONOMIES, DO YOU?
YES, THAT'S RIGHT.
BY MAY 1945 HALDEMAN WAS THE VICE PRESIDENT AND PROVINCIAL SECRETARY OF THE PARTY. HE RAN AS CANDIDATE FOR THE PRINCE ALBERT FEDERAL ELECTORAL DISTRICT IN SASKATCHEWAN BUT WAS UNSUCCESSFUL.
VOTE
X

ONE DAY, WHEN THE HALDEMANS WERE DRIVING FROM REGINA TO CALGARY, THEY SAW A PLANE SITTING IN A FIELD.
FOR

HALDEMAN HAD NO MONEY, BUT HE DID HAVE THE CAR WHICH HE EXCHANGED FOR THE PLANE. THEN HE PUT HIS WIFE ON A TRAIN AND HIRED A PILOT TO FLY BOTH HIM AND THE PLANE BACK TO REGINA.

HE TOOK HIS FIRST FLYING LESSON AT THE AGE OF 45, EARNING HIS LICENSE THE FOLLOWING YEAR IN 1948. HE WAS SOON FLYING ALL OVER NORTH AMERICA, ATTENDING POLITICAL AND CHIROPRACTIC EVENTS.

BY 1950, HALDEMAN HAD TIRED OF CANADA AND WAS LOOKING FOR NEW ADVENTURES. HE MOVED HIS FAMILY TO SOUTH AFRICA, DESPITE NEVER HAVING VISITED THE COUNTRY.

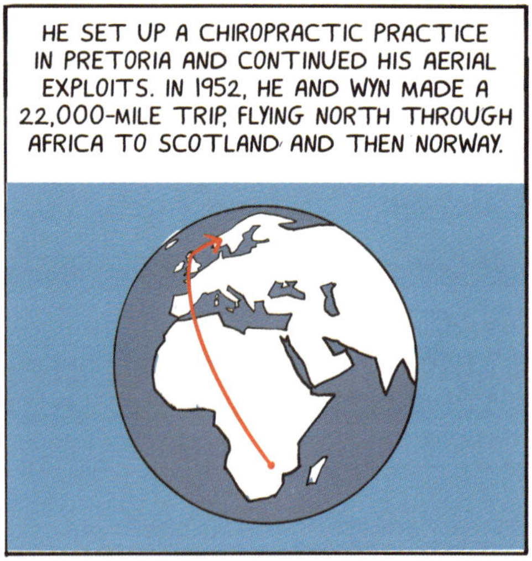
HE SET UP A CHIROPRACTIC PRACTICE IN PRETORIA AND CONTINUED HIS AERIAL EXPLOITS. IN 1952, HE AND WYN MADE A 22,000-MILE TRIP, FLYING NORTH THROUGH AFRICA TO SCOTLAND AND THEN NORWAY.

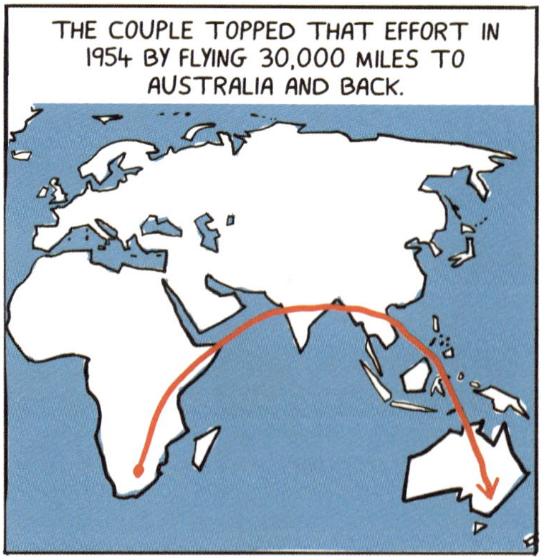
THE COUPLE TOPPED THAT EFFORT IN 1954 BY FLYING 30,000 MILES TO AUSTRALIA AND BACK.

IF THAT WERE NOT ENOUGH, THE HALDEMANS WOULD OFTEN EMBARK ON LONG EXPEDITIONS OUT IN THE DESERT IN SEARCH OF THE LOST CITY OF THE KALAHARI.
HALDEMAN GOT THE IDEA FROM A BOOK WRITTEN BY A CANADIAN NAMED GUILLERMO FARINI (AKA WILLIAM LEONARD HUNT), WHO'D CROSSED THE DESERT IN THE NINETEENTH CENTURY IN A WAGON.
THAT'S ME.
FARINI, WHO, AMONG OTHER EXPLOITS, HAD WALKED OVER NIAGARA FALLS ON A TIGHTROPE, CLAIMED THAT HE'D COME ACROSS THE RUINS OF A GREAT CITY OUT IN THE DESERT.
HALDEMAN FULLY BELIEVED THIS STORY AND WAS DETERMINED TO FIND THE CITY. SOMETIMES HE WOULD TAKE THE PLANE, WHILE HIS WIFE WOULD DRIVE THE CAR.
ON OTHER OCCASIONS THEY WOULD TAKE THE CHILDREN WITH THEM AND SPEND WEEKS IN THE DESERT.
WINNIE

THEY MADE TWELVE EXPEDITIONS ACROSS THE KALAHARI, BUT NEVER FOUND THE FABLED LOST CITY.
APART FROM BEING FLYERS AND EXPLORERS, JOSHUA AND WYN WERE ALSO CRACK SHOT MARKSMEN WHO WON NATIONAL SHOOTING COMPETITIONS.
IN THE MID-1950s THEY ENTERED THE 8,000-MILE CAPE TOWN TO ALGIERS MOTOR RALLY. THE COUPLE OUTDROVE THE PROFESSIONAL RACERS, COMING IN FIRST IN THEIR HUMBLE FORD STATION WAGON.
12
A RECENT ARTICLE IN THE ATLANTIC THROWS SOME LIGHT ONTO WHY HALDEMAN LEFT CANADA FOR SOUTH AFRICA. IT SEEMS THAT HALDEMAN WAS A PRO-APARTHEID, ANTISEMITIC CONSPIRACY THEORIST WHO BLAMED MANY OF THE WORLD'S PROBLEMS ON JEWISH FINANCIERS.
THE TITLE OF HIS 1960 SELF-PUBLISHED TRACT THE INTERNATIONAL CONSPIRACY TO ESTABLISH A WORLD DICTATORSHIP AND THE MENACE TO SOUTH AFRICA, ILLUSTRATES HIS THINKING...
...MERE MONTHS AFTER THE SHARPEVILLE MASSACRE, WHEN SOUTH AFRICAN POLICE SHOT AND KILLED 69 BLACK PROTESTERS.

HE BELIEVED THE INTERNATIONAL MEDIA PAID TOO MUCH ATTENTION TO THE AFRICAN NATIONAL CONGRESS (ANC) AND OTHER ANTI-APARTHEID GROUPS.
ANC
AND HE REPEATEDLY REFERRED TO THE "INTERNATIONAL CONSPIRACY" PULLING THE STRINGS BEHIND IT ALL, WHOM HE COMPLAINED CONTROLLED THE PRESS AND THE MEDICAL PROFESSION.
HALDEMAN ARGUED THAT BLACK SOUTH AFRICANS WERE HAPPY WITH THEIR POSITION UNDER APARTHEID AND EVEN GRATEFUL FOR "THE PROTECTION" OF WHITE PEOPLE.
INTERNATIONAL MEDDLERS ARE TO BLAME FOR RILING UP OPPOSITION.
FOR BETTER OR WORSE, THERE ARE SOME PEOPLE FOR WHOM THE NORMS OF ORDINARY LIFE ARE TOO CONFINING. JOSHUA HALDEMAN WAS A MAN WHO TOOK RISKS. THESE RISKS GENERALLY WORKED OUT UNTIL THE END.
HE DIED IN 1974 AT THE AGE OF 71. THE WHEELS OF HIS PLANE CAUGHT ON A WIRE WHEN LANDING.
THE PLANE FLIPPED. HALDEMAN WAS KILLED IN THE CRASH.

ONE OF HALDEMAN'S TWIN DAUGHTERS, MAYE MUSK, IS ELON MUSK'S MOTHER. AS A TEENAGER MAYE WORKED AS A MODEL. SOMETHING SHE HAS CONTINUED DOING WELL INTO HER SEVENTIES.
IN HER EARLY TWENTIES, SHE WAS A FINALIST IN THE 1969 MISS SOUTH AFRICA BEAUTY COMPETITION.
SHE HAS APPEARED ON THE COVERS OF NUMEROUS MAGAZINES, INCLUDING *TIME MAGAZINE HEALTH EDITION*, *WOMEN'S DAY*, *VOGUE*, *ELLE*, AND *SPORTS ILLUSTRATED'S* SWIMSUIT ISSUE.
SHE PLAYED A ROLE IN A BEYONCÉ MUSIC VIDEO AND HAS BEEN FEATURED IN NUMEROUS ADS FOR BRANDS FROM REVLON TO SPECIAL K CEREAL.
SHE ACHIEVED A DEGREE OF FAME LONG BEFORE HER SON BECAME WELL-KNOWN, BUT IT WAS NOT ALWAYS THAT WAY.
FIRST, SHE RAISED THREE CHILDREN AS A SINGLE MOTHER WHILE EARNING TWO MASTER'S DEGREES AND ESTABLISHING A CAREER AS A DIETITIAN AND NUTRITIONIST.

FROM THE AGE OF SIXTEEN ONWARDS, MAYE MUSK HAD AN ON-AND-OFF RELATIONSHIP WITH THE MAN WHO WOULD BECOME HER HUSBAND AND ELON'S FATHER, ERROL MUSK.
ERROL MUSK RELENTLESSLY PURSUED MAYE. WHEN SHE WAS TWENTY-ONE, HE FOLLOWED HER FROM PRETORIA TO CAPE TOWN WHERE SHE WAS WORKING, AND WHEN SHE TURNED DOWN HIS OFFER OF MARRIAGE...
...HE RETURNED TO PRETORIA AND TOLD HER PARENTS THAT SHE HAD AGREED TO MARRY HIM. A WEDDING WAS ARRANGED AND INVITES WERE SENT OUT. MAYE ONLY LEARNED ABOUT THIS IN A TELEGRAM.
CONGRAT-ULATIONS
A COMBINATION OF SOCIAL PRESSURE AND POOR SELF-CONFIDENCE COERCED HER INTO A MARRIAGE SHE WAS NOT SURE SHE WANTED.
IN HER BOOK, *A WOMAN MAKES A PLAN*, MAYE MUSK GIVES DETAILS OF THE ABUSIVE MARRIAGE SHE FOUND HERSELF IN.
A WOMAN MAKES A PLAN
SHE WROTE THAT HE BEGAN BEATING HER ON THEIR HONEYMOON.

THEY WERE IN EUROPE. SHE WOULD HAVE LEFT, BUT HE HAD HER PASSPORT.
YOU'RE NOT LEAVING.
MAYE MUSK WROTE THAT HER YEARS WITH ERROL MUSK WERE HELL. A TIME SHE DOESN'T CARE TO TALK ABOUT BECAUSE IT WAS SO PAINFUL.
ERROL MUSK HAD THE PERSONALITY TRAITS OF AN ABUSIVE MAN: JEALOUSY, POSSESSIVENESS, UNPREDICTABILITY, VERBAL ABUSE, A VIOLENT TEMPER, AND CONTROLLING BEHAVIOR.
PLUS ALL THE USUAL ANTIQUATED BELIEFS SUCH MEN HAVE ABOUT THE ROLES OF WOMEN AND MEN IN RELATIONSHIPS.
WHEN MAYE'S FATHER DIED, ERROL MUSK WAS IRATE THAT HE WOULD RECIEVE NOTHING IN THE WILL.
I DIDN'T MARRY YOU TO SEE YOUR MOTHER GET ALL THE MONEY.
MAYE'S MOTHER GAVE THE COUPLE THE PLANE AND SOLD THEM THE PLOT OF LAND WHERE THEY HAD BUILT A HOUSE AT LOW COST, BUT ERROL WAS STILL NOT HAPPY. HE DIDN'T LET MAYE SEE HER FAMILY FOR TWO YEARS, AND THEY, IN TURN, WERE NOT ALLOWED TO SEE MAYE'S CHILDREN.

THE PHYSICAL ABUSE ONLY STOPPED AFTER AN INCIDENT WHEN MAYE'S FRIENDS INTERVENED AND TOOK HER TO HER MOTHER'S HOUSE.
WINNIFRED HALDEMAN GAVE ERROL AN ULTIMATUM.
NEVER TOUCH MY DAUGHTER AGAIN, OR SHE'LL BE BACK HERE FOR GOOD.
BUT THE VERBAL ABUSE CONTINUED. ACCORDING TO MAYE, HE THREATENED TO CUT UP HER FACE AND SHOOT THE CHILDREN IN THE KNEES IF SHE EVER DIVORCED HIM. MAYE DID FINALLY LEAVE HIM WHEN SOUTH AFRICAN LAWS CHANGED TO ALLOW "IRRETRIEVABLE BREAKDOWN OF MARRIAGE" AS CAUSE FOR DIVORCE.
SHE MOVED TO DURBAN AND BEGAN A DIETICIAN PRACTICE, SUPPLEMENTED WITH MODELLING WORK.
ERROL HAS PUBLICLY DISPUTED PORTRAYALS OF HIS CHARACTER IN OTHER PUBLICATIONS, NOTABLY WALTER ISAACSON'S BIOGRAPHY OF ELON MUSK.

MAYE MUSK'S CHILDREN.
TOSCA.
ELON.
KIMBAL.
MAYE'S ELDEST CHILD, ELON MUSK.
ACCORDING TO HIS MOTHER, ELON WAS BRILLIANT FROM A VERY EARLY AGE. LIKE A LOT OF SMART KIDS, HE READ VORACIOUSLY. IT WAS NOT UNUSUAL FOR HIM TO READ FOR TEN HOURS STRAIGHT.
ROBERT A. HEINLEIN THE MOON IS A HARSH MISTRESS
WHEN HE WAS AROUND TEN YEARS OLD, HAVING READ ALL THE BOOKS OF INTEREST AT THE SCHOOL LIBRARY, HE BEGAN READING EVERY VOLUME OF THE ENCYCLOPEDIA BRITANNICA.
HE HAD THE ABILITY TO REMEMBER HUGE AMOUNTS OF INFORMATION, AND THIS TURNED HIM INTO A FACT MACHINE THAT DIDN'T ALWAYS ENDEAR HIM TO OTHER CHILDREN.
THE DISTANCE FROM THE EARTH TO THE MOON IS 384,400 KILOMETERS!
THE DISTANCE BETWEEN MY FIST AND YOUR FACE IS A LOT LESS. GEEK.
WHEN HE WAS 12, MUSK CODED AN 8-BIT SHOOTER GAME IN THE STYLE OF *SPACE INVADERS* CALLED *BLASTAR*. THE GAME'S CODE WAS PUBLISHED BY *PC AND OFFICE TECHNOLOGY MAGAZINE*, WHICH PAID MUSK $500.

WHEN HE WAS AROUND TEN, ELON DECIDED THAT HE WANTED TO LIVE WITH HIS FATHER. IT WAS A STRANGE DECISION TO MAKE CONSIDERING HOW ABUSIVE ERROL COULD BE.
PERHAPS PART OF YOUNG ELON'S THINKING WAS THAT HIS FATHER WAS VASTLY BETTER OFF FINANCIALLY THAN HIS MOTHER. AT ERROL'S, ELON WOULD HAVE PLENTY OF BOOKS AND HIS OWN COMPUTER, AND BE TREATED TO OVERSEAS TRIPS.
ERROL RAN A SUCCESSFUL ENGINEERING BUSINESS THAT HANDLED LARGE PROJECTS, SUCH AS RETAIL COMPLEXES, RESIDENTIAL SUBDIVISIONS, AND AN AIR FORCE BASE.
IN A NOTABLE DEAL, ERROL SOLD THE PLANE HE AND MAYE HAD INHERITED FROM HER FATHER FOR A PORTION OF EMERALDS FROM A ZAMBIAN MINE.
IN AN INTERVIEW WITH *BUSINESS INSIDER SOUTH AFRICA*, ERROL WAS QUOTED SAYING THEY HAD SO MUCH MONEY THAT AT TIMES, HE COULDN'T EVEN CLOSE THE SAFE.
ACCORDING TO ERROL, ON A TRIP TO NEW YORK, THE TEENAGE BROTHERS, ELON AND KIMBAL, TRIED THEIR HAND AT SELLING TWO OF THE EMERALDS.

ONE DAY WHILE THEIR FATHER WAS ASLEEP THEY WENT TO TIFFANY AND CO, ON FIFTH AVENUE, ONE OF THE WORLD'S MOST FAMOUS JEWELERS...
...AND SOLD THE TWO EMERALDS. ONE FOR $800 AND THE OTHER FOR $1,200. THIS STORY DOES SEEM UNLIKELY, BUT ERROL MUSK CLAIMS IT'S TRUE.
THE MONEY AND THE FOREIGN TRIPS MUST HAVE BEEN A BIG INDUCEMENT FOR ELON TO MOVE TO HIS FATHER'S.
IT WAS A DECISION HE WOULD REGRET. LIFE WITH HIS DOMINATING FATHER WAS TOUGH. ELON IS RELUCTANT TO DISCUSS THIS PERIOD, BUT IT'S CLEAR THAT HE HAD A MISERABLE TIME. IT'S UNCLEAR IF HIS CHILDREN HAVE EVER BEEN ALLOWED TO MEET THEIR GRANDFATHER.
ELON'S FIRST COMPUTER, BOUGHT BY HIS FATHER, WAS A COMMODORE VIC-20. THE LESSONS ON HOW TO USE THE BASIC PROGRAMMING LANGUAGE WERE SUPPOSED TO TAKE SIX MONTHS, BUT ELON CLAIMS HE BLEW THROUGH THEM OVER THREE DAYS WITHOUT SLEEP.
YET ELON'S TEENAGE LIFE WASN'T ALL BOOKS AND COMPUTERS. THERE WERE MORE DANGEROUS ACTIVITIES. ALONG WITH HIS BROTHER KIMBAL AND COUSINS RUSS, LYNDON, AND PETER RIVE, HE EXPERIMENTED WITH EXPLOSIVES.

IN SOUTH AFRICA, THE BOYS HAD NO ACCESS TO THE FIRECRACKERS AVAILABLE IN OTHER COUNTRIES, SO THEY MADE THEIR OWN CHEMICAL COMPOUNDS FROM HOUSEHOLD ITEMS.
ELON KNEW THAT SALTPETER, SULFUR, AND CHARCOAL WERE THE BASIC INGREDIENTS OF GUNPOWDER, AND THAT IF HE COMBINED A STRONG ACID WITH A STRONG ALKALINE, IT WOULD RELEASE A LOT OF ENERGY.
THE ADULT ELON SAYS HE'S LUCKY TO HAVE ALL HIS FINGERS.
OTHER TEENAGE ACTIVITIES WERE MORE TYPICAL: DIRT BIKING...
...AND DUNGEONS & DRAGONS.
EVEN AT THIS YOUNG AGE, ELON, HIS BROTHER, AND COUSINS WERE ENTREPRENEURIAL. WITHOUT THEIR PARENTS' KNOWLEDGE THEY ATTEMPTED TO START THEIR OWN VIDEO ARCADE.

THEY GOT A LEASE AND BEGAN THE PROCESS OF GETTING THE PERMITS NEEDED FOR THE BUSINESS, BUT IT ALL CAME TO NOTHING WHEN THEY WERE UNABLE TO CONVINCE AN ADULT TO SIGN A LEGAL DOCUMENT FOR THEM.
NOT A CHANCE.

AS A GEEKY KID, MUSK WAS INEVITABLY BULLIED AT SCHOOL. IN ONE INCIDENT HE WAS KICKED IN THE HEAD AND PUSHED DOWN A FLIGHT OF STAIRS. THE ATTACK RESULTED IN A TRIP TO THE HOSPITAL. IT WAS A WEEK BEFORE HE COULD RETURN TO SCHOOL.

IN INTERVIEWS MUSK CLAIMS THAT AT SCHOOL THE BULLYING WAS RELENTLESS AND HE WOULD ARRIVE HOME TO FIND THE SITUATION JUST AS DIFFICULT THERE, ALTHOUGH HE HAS DENIED ERROL WAS EVER PHYSICALLY VIOLENT TOWARD HIM.

HIS SITUATION IMPROVED ONLY AFTER HE MOVED FROM BRYANSTON HIGH SCHOOL TO PRETORIA BOYS HIGH SCHOOL WHERE THE STUDENTS' BEHAVIOUR WAS FAR BETTER.
PHEW! GLAD THAT'S OVER.

FELLOW CLASSMATES REPORT THAT HE WAS QUIET BUT UNREMARKABLE. THERE WERE FOUR OR FIVE STUDENTS WHO WERE THOUGHT TO BE THE BRIGHTEST. ELON MUSK WAS NOT IN THIS GROUP.
MEDIOCRE
HEY MUSK. I THINK YOU BELONG THROUGH THERE.
BRIGHT FUTURE
NOPE.

AFTER GRADUATING FROM PRETORIA HIGH SCHOOL HE ATTENDED THE UNIVERSITY OF PRETORIA, STUDYING PHYSICS AND ENGINEERING. BUT HE DROPPED OUT AFTER ONLY FIVE MONTHS. MUSK HAD OTHER IDEAS ABOUT HIS FUTURE.

HIS PLAN WAS TO MOVE TO CANADA. THE LAW HAD RECENTLY CHANGED TO ALLOW MAYE TO PASS HER CANADIAN CITIZENSHIP ON TO HER CHILDREN. MUSK'S LONG-TERM AIM WAS THE UNITED STATES, BUT CANADA WORKED AS A STEP NEARER.
HIS ENROLLMENT AT THE UNIVERSITY OF PRETORIA SPARED HIM FROM SOUTH AFRICA'S REQUIRED MILITARY SERVICE AND GAVE HIM THE TIME NEEDED TO COMPLETE PAPERWORK FOR A CANADIAN PASSPORT. THE PROCESS TOOK ABOUT A YEAR.
IN JUNE 1989, MUSK LEFT SOUTH AFRICA FOR CANADA. HE WAS SEVENTEEN.
MAYE GAVE HIM THE ADDRESSES OF CANADIAN RELATIVES AND $2,000 IN TRAVELERS CHECKS. SHE ALSO WROTE TO HER FAMILY TO SAY ELON WAS ON HIS WAY.
WHEN ELON ARRIVED IN MONTREAL HE PHONED HIS UNCLE, BUT THERE WAS NO ANSWER. THE UNCLE HAD GONE TO MINNESOTA.
HE RANG HIS MOTHER AND SHE TOLD HIM TO STAY AT A YOUTH HOSTEL.
BELL

HE SPENT A FEW DAYS IN MONTREAL, THEN BOUGHT A BUS TICKET AND SET OFF FOR A SECOND COUSIN'S HOME IN SWIFT CURRENT, SASKATCHEWAN.
SWIFT CURRENT
HI, I'M ELON.
OVER THE NEXT YEAR OR SO, MUSK DID A VARIETY OF MENIAL ODD JOBS. HE WORKED ON HIS COUSIN'S FARM...
...CUT LOGS WITH A CHAINSAW IN VANCOUVER...
...AND CLEANED THE BOILER ROOM OF A LUMBER MILL.
SO HOT IN HERE.

MEANWHILE, MAYE AND HER OTHER CHILDREN, TOSCA AND KIMBAL, WERE ALSO CONSIDERING MOVING TO CANADA.
WE SHOULD GO TOO.
SO KEEN WAS FIFTEEN-YEAR-OLD TOSCA TO MOVE THAT WHILE HER MOTHER WAS IN CANADA CHECKING OUT PLACES TO LIVE, TOSCA PUT THE HOUSE IN SOUTH AFRICA UP FOR SALE.
FOR SALE
BY THE TIME MAYE RETURNED, TOSCA HAD SOLD THE CAR AND THE FURNITURE.
WHAT THE...?
THIS SEEMS TO BE A MUSK FAMILY TRAIT: ACT IMPULSIVELY AND DON'T WORRY ABOUT THE SOCIAL NORMS THAT HOLD OTHER PEOPLE BACK.
THERE'S NO TIME LIKE THE PRESENT.
THE FAMILY—WITH ELON BUT MINUS KIMBAL (WHO WOULD JOIN THEM AFTER HE FINISHED HIS STUDIES IN SOUTH AFRICA)—ENDED UP IN A ONE-BEDROOM APARTMENT IN TORONTO.
I GUESS I'LL SLEEP ON THE COUCH THEN.
IT WAS DECEMBER AND THEY ONLY HAD SUMMER CLOTHES. THEY HAD TO BORROW COATS FROM RELATIVES.

IN 1989 ELON ENROLLED AT QUEEN'S UNIVERSITY IN ONTARIO. IT WAS HERE HE FIRST BEGAN TO SHOW THE INTENSITY AND COMPETITIVENESS HE WOULD LATER BE KNOWN FOR. HE TOOK BUSINESS CLASSES AND COMPETED IN PUBLIC SPEAKING CONTESTS.
HE RAN A SMALL BUSINESS OUT OF HIS DORM, SELLING COMPUTER PARTS AND FULL PCs TO OTHER STUDENTS.
I NEED A SIMPLE WORD PROCESSOR. CAN YOU BUILD THAT? NOTHING FANCY.
OF COURSE.
AFTER TWO YEARS AT QUEEN'S, MUSK TRANSFERRED TO THE UNIVERSITY OF PENNSYLVANIA, WHERE HE RECEIVED A BACHELOR'S DEGREES IN PHYSICS AND ECONOMICS.
HERE HE MET ADEO RESSI, LATER A SUCCESSFUL ENTREPRENEUR AND INVESTOR. THE PAIR FOUND THE CAMPUS SOCIAL SCENE DULL, SO THEY RENTED A TEN-BEDROOM HOUSE AND TURNED IT INTO AN UNOFFICIAL NIGHTCLUB.
THEY SOMETIMES GOT AS MANY AS FIVE HUNDRED PATRONS ON A SINGLE NIGHT, AT $5 A TICKET.
ON ONE OF MAYE'S VISITS, SHE ENDED UP WORKING THE DOOR, ARMING HERSELF WITH A PAIR OF SCISSORS IN CASE OF ROBBERY AS THE MONEY PILED UP IN A SHOE BOX.

WHILE STUDENTS PARTIED AROUND HIM, ELON STAYED SOBER. ACCORDING TO RESSI, MUSK NEVER DRANK OR TOOK ILLICIT SUBSTANCES.
SOMEONE HAD TO RUN THE PARTIES. IT WAS A BUSINESS. A WAY OF PAYING MY RENT.
MUSK'S ADDICTION WAS VIDEO GAMES. HIS SESSIONS WOULD SOMETIMES GO ON FOR DAYS.
HE WROTE A PAPER FOR A BUSINESS CLASS ON SOLAR POWER, WHICH INCLUDED A DRAWING OF AN ORBITAL POWER STATION—A GIANT SOLAR ARRAY IN SPACE THAT WOULD SEND ENERGY BACK TO EARTH VIA MICROWAVE BEAMS.
IN ANOTHER PAPER HE DISCUSSED ULTRACAPACITORS AND THEIR POTENTIAL USE IN ENERGY STORAGE AND HOW THIS COULD BE APPLIED TO CARS, PLANES, AND ROCKETS.
HE WANTED TO EXCEL AFTER COLLEGE. HE BRIEFLY CONSIDERED THE VIDEO GAME BUSINESS BUT THOUGHT HE'D ONLY WASTE HIS TALENT IN AN AREA THAT WOULD HAVE LITTLE EFFECT ON THE WORLD.
I LOVE VIDEO GAMES, BUT THAT'S NOT WHERE MY FUTURE LIES.

HE CONSIDERED THE INTERNET, RENEWABLE ENERGY, AND SPACE TO BE THE THREE FIELDS WITHIN WHICH HE COULD MAKE THE MOST IMPACT ON THE WORLD.
IN 1994 MUSK SPENT THE SUMMER WORKING INTERNSHIPS AT TWO COMPANIES IN SILICON VALLEY.
SAN FRANCISCO
ALAMEDA
SILICON
SANTA CRUZ
SANTA CLARA
HE WORKED DURING THE DAY AT PINNACLE RESEARCH INSTITUTE, A START-UP THAT WAS EXPLORING THE POTENTIAL OF SPACE-BASED WEAPONS, ADVANCED SURVEILLANCE SYSTEMS, AND ALTERNATIVE WAYS OF POWERING CARS.
AND IN THE EVENING HE WOULD MAKE HIS WAY TO ROCKET SCIENCE GAMES, A START-UP THAT WAS ATTEMPTING TO BOOST THE QUALITY OF VIDEO GAMES BY MOVING THEM OFF CARTRIDGES AND ONTO CDs.
AFTER MUSK GRADUATED WITH TWO DEGREES FROM THE UNIVERSITY OF PENNSYLVANIA, HE WAS ACCEPTED INTO A PhD PROGRAM IN MATERIALS SCIENCE AT STANFORD UNIVERSITY IN CALIFORNIA...
...BUT ALLEGEDLY DROPPED OUT AFTER TWO DAYS. SOME HAVE QUESTIONED WHETHER MUSK WAS ACCEPTED TO STANFORD AT ALL. TECHNICALLY HE DIDN'T EVEN ENROLL, BUT STANFORD DOES HAVE A RECORD OF HIS ADMITTANCE.
GOODBYE.

WHAT TRIGGERED HIM TO LEAVE WAS NETSCAPE. THE INTERNET COMPANY THAT OWNED THE THEN-DOMINANT WEB BROWSER HAD JUST GONE PUBLIC WITH A VALUATION OF NEARLY $3 BILLION DOLLARS.
THE INTERNET WAS BOOMING, AND MUSK WANTED TO GET IN AT THE BEGINNING.
I DON'T WANT TO BE LEFT BEHIND.
IN 1995, MUSK AND HIS BROTHER KIMBAL FOUNDED THE WEB SOFTWARE COMPANY ZIP2. THE IDEA WAS TO PROVIDE A SEARCHABLE INTERNET BUSINESS DIRECTORY—AN ONLINE VERSION OF THE YELLOW PAGES TELEPHONE BOOK BUT WITH MAPS INCLUDED.
WE WON'T NEED THIS ANYMORE.
YELLOW PAGES
ASHLEE VANCE'S BIOGRAPHY OF MUSK CLAIMS THE VENTURE WAS PARTLY FUNDED BY ERROL MUSK WHO SUPPLIED ZIP2 WITH $28,000.
LET'S SAY YOU WANTED TO FIND THE NEAREST PIZZA PARLOR. ZIP2 WILL TELL YOU WHERE IT IS AND GIVE YOU TURN-BY-TURN DIRECTIONS TO GET THERE.
THE COMPANY WOULD MAKE MONEY BY CONVINCING LOCAL BUSINESSES TO PAY FOR A SPONSORED LISTING ON ZIP2.
LET YOUR CUSTOMERS FIND YOU.

THE BROTHERS RENTED A SMALL OFFICE IN PALO ALTO. ELON DID THE CODING WHILE KIMBAL HANDLED THE SALES OPERATION.
PALO ALTO
SILICON VALLEY
THEY WERE JOINED AS COFOUNDERS OF ZIP2 BY GREG KOURI, A LEBANESE-CANADIAN BUSINESSMAN WHOM THE BROTHERS HAD MET IN TORONTO. KOURI INVESTED MONEY IN THE COMPANY AND ACTED AS A MENTOR TO THE MUSKS.
HOW WAS IT DONE? THE MUSKS BOUGHT A LICENSE FOR A DATABASE OF BUSINESSES IN THE BAY AREA. THEN THEY CONTACTED NAVTEQ, A COMPANY THAT HAD CREATED A DIGITAL MAP AND DIRECTIONS THAT COULD BE USED IN GPS SYSTEMS...
TRIPLE
EL
ALTO
MIDTOWN
...AND ASKED TO USE THE DATABASE. NAVTEQ GAVE THE MUSKS THIS SOFTWARE ON THE UNDERSTANDING THAT PAYMENT WOULD BE MADE WHEN ZIP2 MADE A PROFIT. ELON THEN BLENDED THE TWO DATABASES TOGETHER, AND ZIP2 WAS BORN.
WE DID IT.
AT FIRST THE MUSKS HAD LITTLE SUCCESS IN SELLING THE ZIP2 CONCEPT TO BUSINESSES. THEY HIRED EXPERIENCED SALES PEOPLE, BUT THEIR RESULTS REMAINED PATCHY.
THE INTERNET IS JUST A FAD. WHY WOULD WE SPEND MONEY ON IT?
Jim's PIZZA
THAT CHANGED IN EARLY 1996 WHEN THE VENTURE CAPITAL FIRM MOHR DAVIDOW VENTURES INVESTED AROUND $3 MILLION DOLLARS IN THE COMPANY.
$

THIS ALLOWED THE MUSKS TO MOVE INTO A LARGER OFFICE AND BEGIN HIRING EXPERIENCED SOFTWARE ENGINEERS.
YOUR CODE IS GOOD, ELON, BUT IT'S CLUMSY. WE'RE GOING TO REWRITE EVERYTHING SO IT'S MORE EFFICIENT.
BUT THE MONEY CAME WITH CONDITIONS. ELON HAD TO CEDE OPERATIONAL CONTROL OF THE COMPANY TO A TECH EXECUTIVE NAMED RICH SORKIN...
CEO
...WHILE MUSK HIMSELF WAS DEMOTED TO CHIEF TECHNOLOGY OFFICER, A MOVE HE WAS SOON TO REGRET.
CTO
AMONGST ZIP2'S FIRST CUSTOMERS WERE *THE NEW YORK TIMES*, *THE CHICAGO TRIBUNE*, AND BIG MEDIA PROPERTIES LIKE THE HEARST CORPORATION. THESE SUCCESSES BROUGHT EVEN MORE MONEY INTO THE COMPANY.
$
$
$
$
IN 1997, ZIP2 HAD ONCE AGAIN OUT-GROWN ITS OFFICES AND HAD TO RELOCATE. THIS TIME TO MOUNTAIN VIEW, CALIFORNIA. BY THEN MUSK HAD BOUGHT HIMSELF AN E-TYPE JAGUAR.
YET HE WAS UNHAPPY. HE'D BEEN SIDELINED IN HIS OWN COMPANY, AND HIS ORIGINAL IDEA FOR ZIP2—OFFERING SERVICES DIRECTLY TO CONSUMERS—WAS BEING IGNORED.
WE WENT IN THE WRONG DIRECTION.

IN 1998, ZIP2 ANNOUNCED THAT IT WOULD MERGE WITH ITS MAIN RIVAL, CITYSEARCH, IN A DEAL WORTH $300 MILLION.
CITY-SEARCH
ZIP2
IN THEORY, THIS LOOKED LIKE A MERGER OF EQUALS, WHERE THE TECHNICIANS OF ZIP2 WOULD COMPLEMENT CITYSEARCH'S SALES AND MARKETING TEAMS.
OH!
CITY-SEARCH
ZIP2
BUT THE DEAL COLLAPSED. IN THE CHAOS THAT FOLLOWED, MUSK URGED THE COMPANY'S BOARD TO SACK RICH SORKIN AND REINSTATE HIMSELF AS CEO.
WELL, THAT DIDN'T WORK.
ZIP2
INSTEAD, SORKIN WAS REPLACED BY DEREK PROUDIAN, A VENTURE CAPITALIST FROM MOHR DAVIDOW, AND MUSK WAS STRIPPED OF HIS CHAIRMAN TITLE.
I'VE BEEN KNOCKED FURTHER DOWN.
ULTIMATELY, ZIP2 WAS SOLD TO COMPAQ IN 1999 FOR $307 MILLION—A HUGE PAYOUT FOR MOHR DAVIDOW, WHICH MADE BACK MORE THAN TWENTY TIMES ITS ORIGINAL INVESTMENT.
$
ELON MADE $22 MILLION AND KIMBAL $15 MILLION FROM THE DEAL.

MUSK NEVER CONSIDERED STAYING ON AT COMPAQ. HE LEFT. HE AIMED TO CREATE AND BUILD A NEW COMPANY AND THIS TIME RETAIN CONTROL. BUT FIRST, HE BEGAN ENJOYING THE FRUITS OF HIS WEALTH. HE BOUGHT A 18,000-SQUARE-FOOT CONDO, A $1 MILLION MCLAREN F1 SPORTS CAR, AND A SMALL PROP PLANE SO HE COULD LEARN TO FLY AS HIS GRANDFATHER HAD BEFORE HIM.
HE POURED $12 MILLION OF HIS OWN MONEY INTO HIS NEXT VENTURE, X.COM, AN ONLINE BANK HE COFOUNDED WITH HARRIS FRICKER, CHRISTOPHER PAYNE, AND ED HO.
FRICKER AND PAYNE WERE CANADIAN FINANCIAL EXPERTS. HO WAS AN ENGINEER WHO MUSK KNEW FROM ZIP2. MUSK WAS THE LARGEST SHAREHOLDER AND THEREFORE THE CEO.
THERE WAS FRICTION ALMOST IMMEDIATELY BETWEEN FRICKER AND MUSK, WHICH CAME TO A HEAD FIVE MONTHS LATER WHEN FRICKER ATTEMPTED TO OUST MUSK FROM HIS POSITION AS CEO.
IN THE END, FRICKER DEPARTED, TAKING PAYNE, HO, AND MANY OF X.COM'S EMPLOYEES WITH HIM. MUSK WAS LEFT WITH BARELY ANY STAFF AND HAD TO START AGAIN.

FOR MUSK IT WAS BACK TO SEEKING INVESTOR FUNDING AND HIRING SILICON VALLEY ENGINEERS. GRADUALLY THE COMPANY SURPASSED WHERE IT HAD BEEN AT THE TIME OF THE SPLIT.
WELCOME, NEW STAFF.
FIRST BY GAINING A BANKING LICENSE AND THEN A MUTUAL FUND LICENSE. BY NOVEMBER 1999, X.COM HAD FORMED A PARTNERSHIP WITH BARCLAYS AND BECAME ONE OF THE FIRST ONLINE BANKS.
ONE OF X.COM'S INNOVATIONS WAS THAT A CUSTOMER COULD SEND MONEY TO ANOTHER PERSON SIMPLY BY TYPING THEIR EMAIL ADDRESS INTO THE SITE.
IN THE FIRST COUPLE OF MONTHS OF OPERATION, MORE THAN TWO HUNDRED THOUSAND PEOPLE SIGNED UP FOR AN X.COM ACCOUNT.
HOWEVER, X.COM WASN'T THE ONLY COMPANY WORKING ON A PEER-TO-PEER PAYMENT SYSTEM.TWO YOUNG ENTREPRENEURS, HAVING LEASED A TINY ROOM IN X.COM'S BUILDING, WERE ALSO GETTING IN ON THE ACT.
WHATEVER THEY'RE DOING IN THERE, WE'VE GOT TO DO IT BETTER.
X.COM
THEIR NAMES WERE MAX LEVCHIN AND PETER THIEL. THEIR START-UP WAS KNOWN AS CONFINITY.

LEVCHIN AND THIEL WERE WORKING ON A WAY OF MOVING MONEY VIA THE INFRARED PORTS ON HANDHELD PALM-PILOTS, THE FIRST POPULAR HANDHELD COMPUTER.
MAKSYMILIAN RAFAILOVYCH "MAX" LEVCHIN WAS BORN IN SOVIET UNION-ERA UKRAINE IN 1975. HE WAS TEN YEARS OLD WHEN THE CHERNOBYL REACTOR EXPLODED LESS THAN A HUNDRED MILES FROM HIS HOME.
HIS PARENTS PUT BOTH HIM AND HIS BROTHER ON A TRAIN. DURING THE JOURNEY A ROSE THORN STUCK IN THE SOLE OF HIS SHOE SET OFF A GEIGER COUNTER.
IN 1991, WHEN MAX WAS SIXTEEN, THE LEVCHIN FAMILY EMIGRATED TO THE UNITED STATES.
THEY ARRIVED AT CHICAGO'S O'HARE INTERNATIONAL AIRPORT WEARING THEIR WINTER COATS TO AVOID HAVING TO DECLARE THEM. IT WAS JULY.
WHEW! IT'S HOT.
LEVCHIN GRADUATED FROM THE UNIVERSITY OF ILLINOIS WITH A BACHELOR'S DEGREE IN COMPUTER SCIENCE IN 1997.

PETER ANDREAS THIEL WAS BORN IN 1967 IN FRANKFURT, IN WHAT WAS THEN WEST GERMANY. HIS FAMILY MOVED TO THE UNITED STATES WHEN HE WAS ONE YEAR OLD.
PETER'S FATHER, KLAUS THIEL, WAS A CHEMICAL ENGINEER WHOSE WORK SOON TOOK THE FAMILY TO NAMIBIA, WHERE HE WORKED ON THE CONSTRUCTION OF A URANIUM MINE.
THE THIELS RETURNED TO THE US WHEN PETER WAS TEN, SETTLING IN FOSTER CITY, CALIFORNIA. PETER HAD THE TYPICAL NERDY CHILDHOOD OF HIGHLY INTELLIGENT KIDS. HE PLAYED "DUNGEONS & DRAGONS", AND READ SCIENCE FICTION AND TOLKIEN.
LORD OF THE RINGS
I'VE READ THIS TEN TIMES.
SIX OF THE FIRMS HE LATER FOUNDED HAD NAMES DERIVED FROM TOLKIEN: PALANTIR TECHNOLOGIES, VALAR VENTURES, MITHRIL CAPITAL, LEMBAS LLC, RIVENDELL LLC, AND ARDA CAPITAL.
NOT THAT I'M OBSESSED WITH IT OR ANYTHING.
AT STANFORD UNIVERSITY HE EARNED A BACHELOR'S DEGREE IN PHILOSOPHY IN 1985, FOLLOWED BY A DOCTORATE IN LAW FROM STANFORD'S LAW SCHOOL IN 1992.
IT'S NOT TRUE THAT I WOULD HAVE PREFERRED WIZARDRY.
WHILE THERE, THIEL PLAYED SPEED CHESS, READ AYN RAND, AND FOUNDED *THE STANFORD REVIEW*, A SMALL RIGHT WING NEWSPAPER CRITICAL OF POLITICAL CORRECTNESS.
DOWN WITH MULTICULTURALISM!

AFTER GRADUATION, THIEL WAS RESTLESS, TRYING OUT DIFFERENT CAREER PATHS. HE WORKED FOR A SHORT WHILE AS A CLERK FOR A REPUBLICAN JUDGE IN ATLANTA.
HE THEN SPENT SEVEN MONTHS AS AN ASSOCIATE IN A SMALL FIRM FOCUSED ON CORPORATE LAW. AFTER THAT HE BECAME A DERIVATIVES TRADER IN CURRENCY OPTIONS AT CREDIT SUISSE.
IT WAS WHILE GIVING A LECTURE AT STANFORD UNIVERSITY THAT HE FIRST MET MAX LEVCHIN. THIEL WAS IMPRESSED BY LEVCHIN AND DECIDED TO INVEST IN THE BUSINESS IDEA HE PROPOSED.
THE DUO ORIGINALLY WORKED ON AN ENCRYPTED WALLET THAT WOULD SECURE A USER'S INFORMATION, INCLUDING MONEY, WHICH COULD BE BEAMED FROM PALM TO PALM.
WE SHOULD CALL THIS PAYPAL.
ULTIMATELY THE PALMPILOT CONCEPT PROVED TO BE A DEAD END. THERE SIMPLY WEREN'T ENOUGH USERS TO MAKE THE PRODUCT WORTHWHILE.
WHAT DID WORK WAS ANOTHER PROPOSAL, WHICH THEY ORIGINALLY THOUGHT WAS JUST A USEFUL ADD-ON, AND CERTAINLY NOT THE BILLION-DOLLAR IDEA IT BECAME.

SENDING MONEY VIA EMAIL. THIS WAS MEANT TO BE A BACKUP TO THE PALMPILOT MONEY-BEAMING OPTION, NOT A REPLACEMENT FOR THEIR ORIGINAL IDEA, WHICH FOR SOME TIME THEY STILL HAD BELIEF IN.
I STILL THINK WE CAN MAKE THIS WORK.
PALM PILOT
MEANWHILE, ELON MUSK WAS BEING TYPICALLY AMBITIOUS. HE WANTED X.COM TO BECOME AN ONLINE BANKING SUPERSITE, THE AMAZON OF BANKS, WHICH WOULD HANDLE ALL OF A CUSTOMER'S FINANCIAL NEEDS...
...INCLUDING LOANS, MORTGAGES, INSURANCE, BANK ACCOUNTS, MUTUAL FUNDS, AND STOCK HOLDINGS.
THE SYSTEM WOULD USE EMAIL AS THE BACKBONE OF ITS SERVICES.
SEND
AND JUST LIKE THEIR RIVALS AT CONFINITY, MUSK AND THE STAFF AT X.COM THOUGHT OF EMAIL PAYMENT AS AN ADD-ON. IT WAS A SURPRISE TO THEM WHEN PEOPLE GOT EXCITED ABOUT IT.
WHAT? YOU CAN SEND MONEY TO ANYWHERE IN THE WORLD FROM A COMPUTER? AMAZING!
FOR BOTH X.COM AND CONFINITY THE EMAIL PAYMENT SYSTEM SOON DEVELOPED POSSIBILITIES FAR BEYOND THOSE ITS CREATORS ENVISAGED, AND THAT WAS MOSTLY BECAUSE OF...
EBAY.
EBAY

EBAY WAS FOUNDED BY FRENCH-BORN PIERRE MORAD OMIDYAR. THE SITE BEGAN IN 1995 AS A SMALL ONLINE AUCTION SERVICE ON HIS PERSONAL WEB PAGE.
I WANTED TO SELL A BROKEN LASER POINTER AND WAS SURPRISED WHEN IT SOLD.
BUT THEN COLLECTORS OF BARBIE DOLLS, BEANIE BABIES, AND HOUSEHOLD JUNK OF ALL SORTS BEGAN TO USE THE SITE UNTIL IT SOON OUTGREW OMIDYAR'S PERSONAL INTERNET ACCOUNT.
I BETTER MOVE THIS TO A PROPER BUSINESS SITE AND CHARGE A SMALL FEE FOR EACH LISTING AND TRANSACTION TO COVER MY COSTS.
EBAY'S GROWTH LED OMIDYAR TO LEAVE HIS DAY JOB AND DEDICATE HIS FULL ATTENTION TO THE ENTERPRISE.
FOUR YEARS LATER, EBAY WAS A BILLION-DOLLAR PUBLICLY TRADED COMPANY.
$1,000,000,000
IN 1999 EBAY ACQUIRED THE PAYMENTS START-UP BILLPOINT WITH THE AIM OF TURNING BILLPOINT INTO ITS DEFAULT PAYMENT SYSTEM.
I'LL BUY THIS.
BILLPoint

BUT EBAY STRUGGLED TO INTEGRATE BILLPOINT INTO ITS SYSTEM.
BILLpoint
EBAY'S CUSTOMERS FOUND OTHER WAYS TO PAY: CHECKS, MONEY ORDERS, WIRE TRANSFERS, AND ONLINE PAYMENT METHODS LIKE X.COM AND PAYPAL.
$
THE BATTLE FOR DOMINANCE OF THE ONLINE PAYMENT MARKET THEN INTENSIFIED.
PAYPAL
X.COM
PAYPAL GAVE ME $10 WHEN I SIGNED UP, PLUS A FURTHER $10 TO PASS ON TO A FRIEND, WHICH THEY KEPT IF THEY SIGNED UP TOO.
AND WHEN THEY DID, I GOT PAID ANOTHER $10 FOR THE REFERRAL. IT'S A SWEET DEAL.
IN THIS WAY CONFINITY CREATED EXPONENTIAL GROWTH FOR PAYPAL.

OVER AT X.COM, MUSK WAS TRYING SIMILAR TACTICS. CUSTOMERS GOT A $20 CASH CARD FOR SIGNING UP AND A $10 CARD FOR EACH ADDITIONAL PERSON THEY SIGNED UP.
GREAT. EVEN MORE FREE MONEY. I'LL SIGN UP FOR BOTH.
BOTH COMPANIES WERE SOON SPENDING TENS OF MILLIONS OF DOLLARS TO CAPTURE MARKET SHARE AND LOSING MILLIONS MORE FIGHTING HACKERS WHO WERE DEFRAUDING THEIR SERVICES.
IT WAS A BRUTAL FIGHT TO SEE WHO COULD SPEND THE MOST MONEY TO DESTROY THE OTHER.
UGH!
GAH!
PAYPAL
X.COM
MUSK COMMITTED HIMSELF FULLY TO THIS WAR. HE'D INVESTED MILLIONS IN HIS COMPANY AND HE NOW WAS WATCHING THAT MONEY BURN UP.
BY EARLY 2000, IT WAS CLEAR THAT A MERGER WAS THE BEST OPTION FOR THE TWO COMPANIES, AND TALKS BEGAN. CONFINITY HAD THE BETTER PRODUCT IN PAYPAL, BUT THEY WERE SPENDING $100,000 A DAY AND SOON RAN OUT OF FUNDS.
X.COM
HOW ABOUT WE BUY CONFINITY AND YOU GET 8 PERCENT OF THE COMBINED VALUE OF THE TWO COMPANIES?
NOT A CHANCE.
CONFINITY

WHILE X.COM NEEDED PAYPAL.
X.COM
OKAY. WHAT ABOUT IF YOU GET 45 PERCENT OF THE COMBINED COMPANY?
I DON'T CARE FOR THE FACT THAT WE'D STILL BE THE JUNIOR PARTNER. SO, NO.
HOW ABOUT FIFTY-FIFTY?
IT'S A DEAL.
IT WAS AN UNEASY MERGER THAT MUSK DIDN'T WANT. THE MAN HE'D HIRED TO BE CEO OF X.COM, BILL HARRIS, PREVIOUSLY CEO OF INTUIT, THREATENED TO QUIT IF THE MERGER DIDN'T HAPPEN.
IT'S BEST FOR THE COMPANY.
THIS WOULD HAVE BEEN DISASTROUS WHEN WE NEEDED TO RAISE MORE FUNDS FROM INVESTORS.
ONE DAY, MUSK TOOK PETER THIEL FOR A RIDE IN HIS MCLAREN. THEY WERE ON THEIR WAY TO A MEETING TO DISCUSS THE MERGER...

WHEN, WHILE SHOWING OFF THE MCLAREN'S SPEED...
WATCH THIS.
...HE CRASHED THE CAR.
THE TWO MEN WERE UNHURT, DESPITE THIEL NOT WEARING A SEATBELT.
I HADN'T INSURED THE CAR.
FOR TWO YEARS PRIOR TO THE MERGER OF CONFINITY AND X.COM, INVESTMENTS IN INTERNET-BASED COMPANIES SOARED.
AS DID THE VALUE OF TECHNOLOGY STOCKS. BUT ALL THIS WAS TO END IN THE SPRING OF 2000 WHEN THE DOT-COM BUBBLE BURST.

THIS WAS ALSO A CRASH THAT MUSK AND THIEL SURVIVED, BUT ONLY JUST. THEY GOT LUCKY. JUST DAYS AFTER THE COMPANY CLOSED AN INVESTMENT ROUND THAT RAISED $100 MILLION, US PUBLIC MARKETS BEGAN FALLING IN A SLIDE THAT WIPED $2.5 TRILLION OFF THE VALUE OF TECHNOLOGY BUSINESS STOCKS. MANY OTHER DOT-COM COMPANIES DID NOT SURVIVE.
GEAR .COM
PETS .COM
BOO .COM
KOZMO .COM
HOME GROCER .COM
THE DOWNTURN ALSO KILLED OFF OTHER ONLINE MONEY SERVICES, CLEARING THE FIELD OF PAYPAL'S RIVALS.
FINISH
WE WON.
HOWEVER, AFTER THE MERGER, ALL WAS NOT WELL INSIDE THE NEW COMPANY.
OR DID WE?
X PayPal
THERE WAS FRICTION BETWEEN THIEL AND CEO BILL HARRIS. THIS LED TO THIEL RESIGNING FROM HIS POSITION AS EXECUTIVE VICE PRESIDENT OF FINANCE.
IT'S NOT ENTIRELY GOODBYE.
I'M STILL ON THE BOARD.
HARRIS WAS NOT A TECH GUY. HE'D BEEN BROUGHT IN FROM THE WORLD OF FINANCE TO PUT X.COM ON A MORE SERIOUS BUSINESS FOOTING.

THIS HE HAD DONE, BUT NOT WITHOUT CAUSING RESENTMENT FROM THE TECH GUYS WHO'D CREATED THE TWO MERGED COMPANIES.
IT WAS THE VIEW OF MANY THAT POST-MERGER GROWTH AND DEVELOPMENT HAD SLOWED TO A RATE THAT RISKED THE COMPANY'S FUTURE.
TOO MANY MEETINGS AND NOT ENOUGH ACTION.
NOT ONLY THAT, BUT MUSK WAS UNHAPPY WITH THE WAY HE'D BEEN STRONG-ARMED BY HARRIS INTO ACCEPTING THE MERGER.
BAH!
HARRIS' STAID PROFESSIONAL BANKING APPROACH WAS AT ODDS WITH THE LOOSE ANYTHING-GOES CULTURE OF THE ORIGINAL START-UP CREW.
AT A BOARD MEETING IN MAY 2000, HARRIS WAS OBLIGED TO RESIGN AND MUSK BECAME CEO.
GO!
ONE OF MUSK'S FIRST ACTS WAS TO APPOINT PETER THIEL CHAIRMAN OF THE BOARD OF DIRECTORS.
I'M BACK, THOUGH I NEVER REALLY LEFT.

BUT STILL ALL WAS NOT WELL INSIDE THE NEWLY MERGED COMPANY.
X.COM
FIRSTLY, MUSK WANTED TO KEEP THE X.COM BRAND, EVEN THOUGH THE PAYPAL NAME WAS GETTING WIDER PUBLIC RECOGNITION.
X.COM SOUNDS LIKE A PORN SITE.
AND SECONDLY, MUSK WANTED TO MOVE THE COMPANY'S TECHNOLOGICAL INFRASTRUCTURE AWAY FROM OPEN-SOURCE SOFTWARE (PAYPAL WAS BUILT USING THE LINUX OPERATING SYSTEM)...
...AND SWITCH OVER TO MICROSOFT WINDOWS, WHICH HE FELT WAS MORE ROBUST.
YOW!
THIS UPSET MAX LEVCHIN AND THE OTHER DEVELOPERS WHO HAD CREATED PAYPAL. THEY SAW LINUX AS A SOFTWARE OF THE PEOPLE AND MICROSOFT AS THE PRODUCT OF A MULTIBILLION-DOLLAR CORPORATION.
WE DON'T WANT TO USE THIS CORPORATE-OWNED SOFTWARE. WE WANT TO BE FREE.

ON TOP OF THIS, THERE WERE SEVERE FINANCIAL PRESSURES ON THE COMPANY. THERE WAS MORE FRAUD, FEES FROM BANKS AND CREDIT CARD COMPANIES WERE SOARING, AND THERE WAS NO CLEAR BUSINESS MODEL TO OFFSET THESE LOSSES AND MAKE A PROFIT.

IN JANUARY 2000 MUSK MARRIED HIS LONGTIME GIRLFRIEND JUSTINE WILSON, WHOM HE'D MET AT QUEEN'S UNIVERSITY IN ONTARIO. MUSK WAS TOO BUSY FOR A HONEYMOON. IT WASN'T UNTIL SEPTEMBER THAT THE COUPLE MANAGED TO GET AWAY, FLYING OFF TO SYDNEY, AUSTRALIA, TO CATCH THE OLYMPICS.

EVEN AS MUSK BOARDED THE PLANE, A COUP WAS BEING ORGANIZED AGAINST HIM.

AFTER FAILING TO CONVINCE MUSK TO ABANDON THE SWITCH TO MICROSOFT AND KEEP THE PAYPAL NAME PROMINENT, THE EXECUTIVE TEAM DELIVERED AN ULTIMATUM TO THE X.COM BOARD.
WE WANT MUSK OUT.

MUSK WAS THEN FIRED FROM HIS POSITION AS CEO...
...AND REPLACED BY PETER THIEL.
BY JUNE 2001, THIEL HAD REBRANDED X.COM AS PAYPAL.
X.COM
AND JUST OVER A YEAR LATER, IN JULY 2002, EBAY BOUGHT PAYPAL FOR $1.5 BILLION.
ebay
PayPal
AS PAYPAL'S LARGEST SHAREHOLDER, MUSK MADE $250 MILLION FROM THE SALE.
MORE THAN ENOUGH TO OFFSET BEING KICKED OUT OF HIS OWN COMPANY AND MAKE FURTHER DREAMS POSSIBLE.
THE FUTURE

TESLA AND SPACEX

SHORTLY AFTER MUSK'S ABRUPT EXIT FROM PAYPAL, HE HAD AN EVEN WORSE EXPERIENCE WHEN HE ALMOST DIED FROM THE FALCIPARUM FORM OF MALARIA.
CONTRACTED ON A TRIP TO BRAZIL AND SOUTH AFRICA WITH JUSTINE IN DECEMBER 2000, THE ILLNESS WAS MISDIAGNOSED.
YOU HAVE MENINGITIS.
HE SPENT TEN DAYS IN INTENSIVE CARE. HE LOST OVER FORTY POUNDS DURING THE COURSE OF THE ILLNESS, LEAVING HIM WITH A CLOSET FULL OF CLOTHES THAT NO LONGER FIT.
IT TOOK FIVE MONTHS FOR HIM TO RECOVER.
ELON MUSK TURNED THIRTY THAT YEAR. HE AND JUSTINE LEFT PALO ALTO AND BY EARLY 2002 HAD BOUGHT A HOUSE IN LOS ANGELES.
EVER SINCE HE WAS A BOY, MUSK'S DREAM HAD BEEN SPACE. HE'D MOVED TO LOS ANGELES TO BE CLOSER TO THE SPACE INDUSTRY AND WAS DESPERATE TO BE INVOLVED.

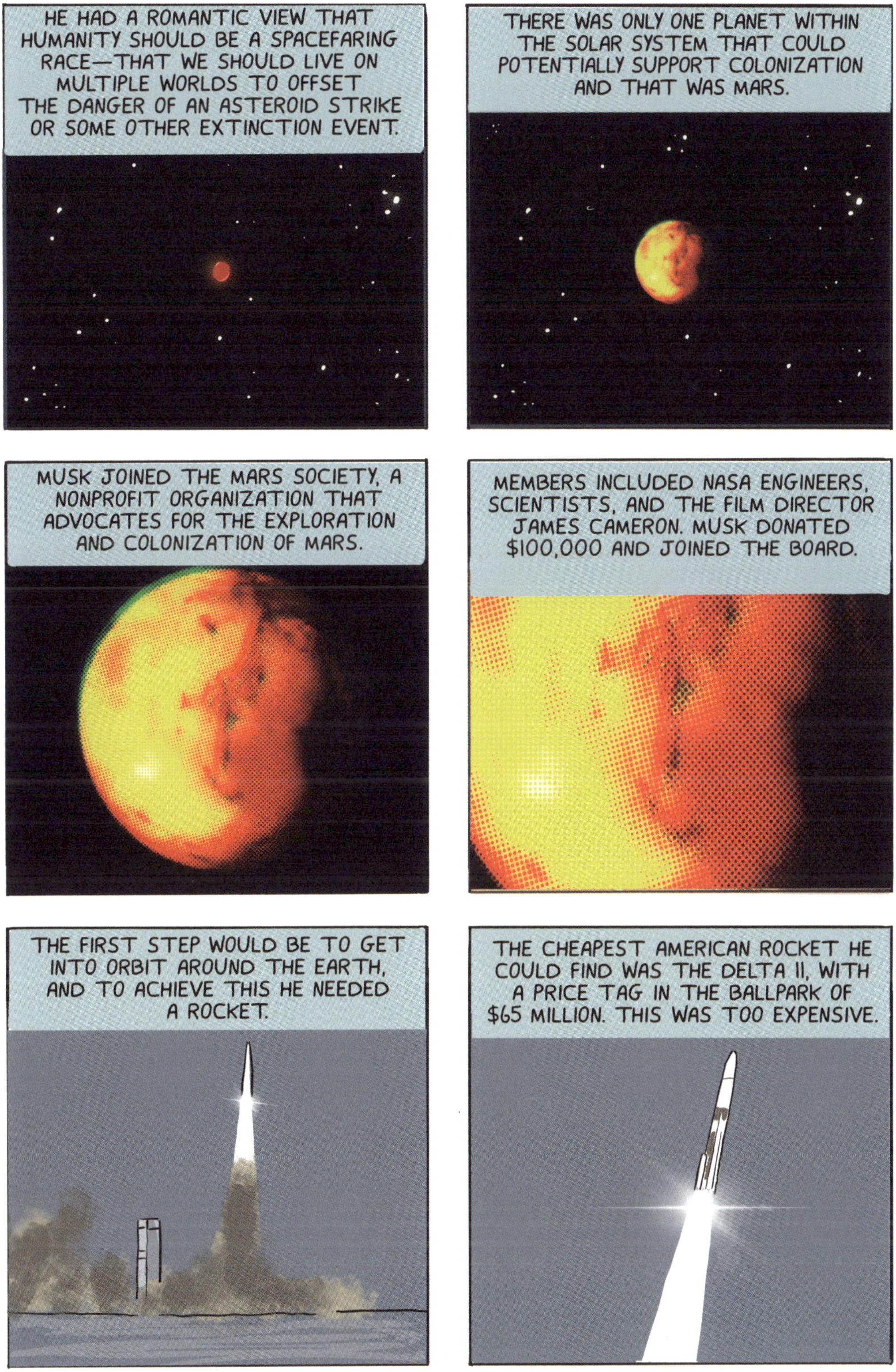
HE HAD A ROMANTIC VIEW THAT HUMANITY SHOULD BE A SPACEFARING RACE—THAT WE SHOULD LIVE ON MULTIPLE WORLDS TO OFFSET THE DANGER OF AN ASTEROID STRIKE OR SOME OTHER EXTINCTION EVENT.
THERE WAS ONLY ONE PLANET WITHIN THE SOLAR SYSTEM THAT COULD POTENTIALLY SUPPORT COLONIZATION AND THAT WAS MARS.
MUSK JOINED THE MARS SOCIETY, A NONPROFIT ORGANIZATION THAT ADVOCATES FOR THE EXPLORATION AND COLONIZATION OF MARS.
MEMBERS INCLUDED NASA ENGINEERS, SCIENTISTS, AND THE FILM DIRECTOR JAMES CAMERON. MUSK DONATED $100,000 AND JOINED THE BOARD.
THE FIRST STEP WOULD BE TO GET INTO ORBIT AROUND THE EARTH, AND TO ACHIEVE THIS HE NEEDED A ROCKET.
THE CHEAPEST AMERICAN ROCKET HE COULD FIND WAS THE DELTA II, WITH A PRICE TAG IN THE BALLPARK OF $65 MILLION. THIS WAS TOO EXPENSIVE.

HE FLEW TO RUSSIA AT LEAST TWICE IN AN ATTEMPT TO BUY A REFURBISHED INTERCONTINENTAL BALLISTIC MISSILE, BUT THAT WAS PRICY TOO, AND THE RUSSIANS DID NOT TAKE HIM SERIOUSLY.
YOU'RE JUST A RICH MAN WHO WANTS TO PLAY WITH ROCKETS.
OH YEAH! GOODBYE.
MUSK REALISED HE WOULD HAVE TO BUILD A ROCKET HIMSELF.
THROUGH A MUTUAL FRIEND HE MET ROCKET ENGINEER TOM MUELLER AND INVITED HIM TO BECOME A BUSINESS PARTNER.
MUELLER WAS THE SON OF A LOGGER IN THE SMALL IDAHO TOWN OF ST. MARIES.
AS A KID, HE BOUGHT MAIL-ORDER ROCKETS AND EVEN MADE ONE OUT OF HIS FATHER'S OXYACETYLENE WELDING EQUIPMENT.
FOR FIFTEEN YEARS, MUELLER WORKED FOR TRW INC, WHERE HE WAS LEAD ENGINEER DURING THE DEVELOPMENT OF THE TR-106 HYDROGEN ENGINE.
TRW

IN MUSK'S VIEW, THERE HAD BEEN NO ADVANCES IN ROCKET TECHNOLOGY IN FIFTY YEARS. THE AEROSPACE COMPANIES WERE STILL BUILDING ENORMOUSLY EXPENSIVE PRODUCTS WHEN CHEAPER AND LEANER WOULD BE MORE EFFECTIVE.
BOEING
SPACE X
WE CAN DO BETTER.
SPACEX WOULD BUILD ITS OWN ENGINES, USING THE ADVANCES IN MATERIALS AND COMPUTING POWER THAT HAD TAKEN PLACE OVER THE PAST FEW DECADES.
LAUNCHED FROM A MOBILE SITE, THE NEW ROCKET WOULD BE ABLE TO TAKE OFF FROM EITHER HORIZONTAL OR VERTICAL POSITIONS.
THIS IS DEFINITELY GOING TO HAPPEN.
SPACEX WOULD MAKE MULTIPLE LAUNCHES A MONTH AND NEVER NEED TO BE A CONTRACTOR DEPENDENT ON GOVERNMENT FUNDS.
CAN YOU PUT OUR SATELLITE IN ORBIT? BECAUSE IF YOU CAN WE'LL HAVE MORE WORK FOR YOU.
OF COURSE.
MUSK ANNOUNCED THAT SPACEX'S FIRST ROCKET WOULD BE CALLED FALCON 1, A REFERENCE TO THE MILLENNIUM FALCON FROM THE MOVIE *STAR WARS*.
IS THIS WHAT IT LOOKS LIKE?
NO.
IN A TIME WHEN THE COST OF A 550-POUND PAYLOAD BEGAN AT $30 MILLION, FALCON 1 WOULD BE ABLE TO CARRY A 1,400-POUND PAYLOAD FOR A MERE $6.9 MILLION.
CHEAP

THEN A PERSONAL TRAGEDY OCCURRED. ELON AND JUSTINE'S FIRST CHILD, NEVADA ALEXANDRA MUSK, WAS BORN IN 2002, BUT LIVED ONLY TEN WEEKS...
...DYING OF SUDDEN INFANT DEATH SYNDROME.
THE PARENTS HAD TUCKED THE BOY IN FOR A NAP, LEAVING HIM ON HIS BACK. WHEN THEY RETURNED, HE WAS NO LONGER BREATHING.
PARAMEDICS RESUSCITATED THE BABY, BUT BRAIN DEATH HAD TAKEN PLACE AND HE DIED AFTER THREE DAYS ON LIFE SUPPORT.
IN A 2010 *MARIE CLAIRE* ARTICLE, JUSTINE WROTE ABOUT HOW ELON REFUSED TO TALK ABOUT NEVADA'S DEATH.
HE CONSIDERED JUSTINE'S OPEN EXPRESSIONS OF GRIEF TO BE "EMOTIONALLY MANIPULATIVE."

MUSK HAS SAID THAT, FROM HIS POINT OF VIEW, WALLOWING IN SADNESS DID NO GOOD. HE HAD TOO MANY OBLIGATIONS AND AMBITIONS TO LET GRIEF GET IN THE WAY. HE THREW HIMSELF INTO HIS WORK. THERE WAS ANOTHER BUSINESS IDEA HE WANTED TO EXPLORE: ELECTRIC CARS.
MEANWHILE, BACK IN SILICON VALLEY, TWO OTHER MEN WERE ALSO THINKING ABOUT ELECTRIC CARS. THEIR NAMES WERE MARTIN EBERHARD AND MARC TARPENNING.
EBERHARD AND TARPENNING WERE BOTH TALENTED ENGINEERS WHO IN 1997 HAD FOUNDED NUVOMEDIA, A COMPANY THAT WENT ON TO CREATE ONE OF THE FIRST POCKET E-READERS, THE ROCKET EBOOK.
IN MARCH 2000, NUVOMEDIA WAS BOUGHT OUT BY GEMSTAR INTERNATIONAL GROUP, THE OWNERS OF *TV GUIDE*, FOR $187 MILLION.
THANK YOU.
THE ROCKET EBOOK DIDN'T BECOME THE COMMERCIAL SUCCESS THAT THE LATER KINDLE DID, BUT IT DID SUCCEED IN MAKING EBERHARD AND TARPENNING WEALTHY...

...AND THEY LEARNED A GOOD DEAL ABOUT LITHIUM-ION BATTERIES, USED TO POWER LAPTOPS AND OTHER PORTABLE DEVICES.
CHARGE
DISCHARGE
ANODE
CATHODE
SEPARATOR
EBERHARD WANTED TO BUY A SPORTS CAR, BUT ENVIRONMENTAL CONCERNS MADE HIM THINK TWICE ABOUT BUYING A REGULAR GAS-GUZZLING CAR.
WAS THERE AN ALTERNATIVE? ELECTRIC CARS SEEMED LIKE THE ANSWER. BUT WHAT WAS AVAILABLE? A TINY LOS ANGELES COMPANY CALLED AC PROPULSION WAS SELLING A LEAD-ACID BATTERY KIT CAR, THE TZERO, THAT COULD ACCELERATE FROM ZERO TO SIXTY MILES AN HOUR IN AROUND FOUR SECONDS.
AC PROPULSION WAS RUN BY ENGINEER ALAN COCCONI, WHO HAD BEEN A DESIGNER ON GENERAL MOTORS' SHORT-LIVED EV1/IMPACT ELECTRIC CARS IN THE 1990S.
EBERHARD ALLEGEDLY OFFERED TO BAIL OUT AC PROPULSION'S DEBTS WITH $500,000 IF THEY BUILT ONE OF THEIR CARS FOR HIM WITH LITHIUM-ION BATTERY CELLS INSTEAD OF LEAD-ACID BATTERIES.
I'LL DO IT. WE WERE MAKING THAT BATTERY CHANGE ANYWAY.

EBERHARD BELIEVED THERE WAS A MARKET FOR A HIGH-END ELECTRIC SPORTS CAR FOR THE RICH AND ECO-LOGICALLY CONSCIOUS.
HE RESEARCHED THE IDEA WITH TARPENNING. THEY DISCOVERED THAT BUYERS OF GREEN CARS TENDED TO BE WEALTHY ENOUGH TO BUY ANYTHING THEY WANTED.
LET'S DO IT.
ON JULY 1, 2003, EBERHARD AND TARPENNING INCORPORATED THEIR NEW COMPANY, CALLING IT TESLA, AFTER THE ELECTRICAL ENGINEER AND INVENTOR NIKOLA TESLA.
THAT'S ME.
NEXT THEY NEEDED FUNDING, BUT THEY STRUGGLED TO FIND INVESTORS. ALMOST THE ONLY PERSON INTERESTED WAS ELON MUSK.
MUSK INVESTED $6.35 MILLION IN TESLA, BECOMING THE LARGEST SHAREHOLDER AND CHAIRMAN OF THE COMPANY'S BOARD OF DIRECTORS.
EBERHARD LATER REALIZED IT HAD BEEN A MISTAKE TO GIVE MUSK SUCH POWER, BUT AT THE TIME, HE HAD NO CHOICE. TESLA NEEDED THE MONEY.

MUSK INTRODUCED TARPENNING AND EBERHARD TO JB STRAUBEL, A STANFORD GRADUATE, WHO'D ALSO BEEN WORKING ON ARRAYS OF LITHIUM-ION BATTERIES TO POWER CARS.
STRAUBEL WOULD BECOME TESLA'S CHIEF TECHNOLOGY OFFICER AND STAY IN THAT ROLE FOR FIFTEEN YEARS.
OTHER ENGINEERS WERE HIRED UNTIL THEY HAD A TEAM OF EIGHTEEN PEOPLE. PREMISES WERE FOUND IN A TWO-STORY INDUSTRIAL BUILDING IN SAN CARLOS.
TESLA MOTORS
THE PLAN WAS TO TAKE A LOTUS ELISE BODY, LICENSE AC PROPULSION'S POWER SYSTEM, AND THEN DESIGN AND BUILD THEIR OWN ELECTRONICS, MOTOR, AND OTHER DRIVETRAIN COMPONENTS.
IT TOOK FOUR MONTHS, BUT BY JANUARY 27, 2005, THE FIRST TESLA PROTOTYPE HAD BEEN BUILT.
TESLA RAISED $13 MILLION IN THE NEXT FUNDING ROUND. NINE MILLION CAME FROM MUSK. THE AIM WAS TO DELIVER THE FIRST CAR TO CONSUMERS IN 2006.
WE DID IT.

HOWEVER, THE LOTUS ELISE CHASSIS WAS CONSIDERED A POOR FIT FOR WHAT TESLA WANTED TO PRODUCE. THE CAR NEEDED TO BE LONGER TO MAKE ROOM FOR THE BATTERY PACK AND A TRUNK.
REJECTED
A SECOND PROTOTYPE—KNOWN AS THE EP1 OR ROADSTER—WAS THEN BUILT.
THE ROADSTER'S GOOD LOOKS AND ZERO-TO-60 MPH ACCELERATION IN ABOUT FOUR SECONDS IMPRESSED, BUT THE CAR WAS FAR FROM PERFECT.
OUT OF SIGHT OF POTENTIAL INVESTORS, THE ROADSTER'S BATTERIES HAD TO BE COOLED DOWN WITH GALLONS OF ICE WATER.
LOOK AT IT GO!
NEVERTHELESS, THE NEXT ROUND OF FUNDING BROUGHT IN $40 MILLION, OF WHICH $12 MILLION WAS MUSK'S.
UNITED STATES OF MUSK
$12 MILLION
A THIRD PROTOTYPE WAS THEN BUILT, AND IN JULY 2006, BOTH ROADSTERS WERE SHOWN AT AN EVENT IN SANTA CLARA.

ATTENDEES WERE TOLD THAT A $100,000 DEPOSIT WOULD BUY THEM ONE OF THE FIRST ROADSTERS OFF THE PRODUCTION LINE.
DELIVERIES WILL BEGIN NEXT SUMMER.
EBERHARD EXPLAINED TESLA'S STRATEGY IN A PROFILE OF THE COMPANY IN *THE NEW YORK TIMES*.
WE'RE GOING TO START WITH EXPENSIVE SPORTS CARS AND THEN MOVE TO MORE AFFORDABLE MODELS AS THE TECHNOLOGY MATURES.
THE *TIMES* PIECE WAS GOOD EXPOSURE, BUT MUSK WAS ANNOYED BY THE FACT THAT HIS NAME HAD BEEN LEFT OUT OF THE ARTICLE.
WHAT?
EVEN WORSE, THE *TIMES* HAD MISTAKENLY REFERRED TO EBERHARD AS CHAIRMAN, WHICH WAS MUSK'S TITLE.
BAH!
OVERALL, MUSK FELT THAT PUBLIC PERCEPTION OF HIS ROLE AT TESLA WAS INACCURATE. HE WAS MORE THAN JUST THE COMPANY'S FINANCIER, AND HE WANTED THE MEDIA TO BE AWARE OF THIS.
IF IT HAPPENS AGAIN I'LL FIRE OUR COMPANY'S PR FIRM.
FROM THIS POINT, THE RELATIONSHIP BETWEEN MUSK AND EBERHARD BEGAN TO DETERIORATE.

IN HER *MARIE CLAIRE ARTICLE*, JUSTINE MUSK WROTE THAT AFTER THEIR SON'S DEATH, BOTH SHE AND ELON WANTED A CHILD AGAIN AS SOON AS POSSIBLE.
THROUGH IN VITRO FERTILIZATION, SHE GAVE BIRTH TO FIVE CHILDREN: TWINS IN 2004 AND TRIPLETS IN 2006.
SHE ALSO BECAME A PUBLISHED NOVELIST, SELLING THREE NOVELS TO PENGUIN AND SIMON & SCHUSTER.
BUT SHE WAS UNHAPPY. ELON WAS A PRODUCT OF THE MALE-DOMINATED CULTURE OF SOUTH AFRICA, AND IN HER VIEW, THE ATTRIBUTES THAT MADE HIM SUCCESSFUL IN BUSINESS DID NOT MAKE FOR A HAPPY MARRIAGE.
I'M NOT YOUR EMPLOYEE.
IF YOU WERE MY EMPLOYEE, I WOULD FIRE YOU.
SHE HAD BECOME THE TROPHY WIFE OF A WEALTHY MAN. HER LIFE CONSISTED OF LOOKING BEAUTIFUL, SHOPPING, AND OVERSEEING DOMESTIC DETAILS.
I WANT YOU TO GO BLONDE.
THE COUPLE DIVORCED IN 2008.

WHILE MUSK WAS DEVELOPING TESLA, HE REMAINED COMMITTED TO SPACEX. BY 2003, IT WAS CLEAR THAT IF SPACEX WERE TO SUCCEED IT NEEDED NASA CONTRACTS.
SPACEX
1310
BUT NOT MANY IN GOVERNMENT OR AT NASA TOOK SPACEX SERIOUSLY.
WHO IS THIS ELON MUSK WHO KEEPS EMAILING ME?
HE'S A RICH GUY WITH A TOY ROCKET COMPANY.
NASA
MUSK ARRANGED A PR STUNT TO GET THEIR ATTENTION. THAT YEAR, THE FEDERAL AVIATION ADMINISTRATION (FAA) PLANNED TO CELEBRATE THE CENTENARY OF THE WRIGHT BROTHERS' FIRST FLIGHT WITH AN EVENT AT THE NATIONAL AIR AND SPACE MUSEUM. MUSK HAD THE ENORMOUS FALCON ROCKET PUT ON A TRAILER, DRIVEN ACROSS THE COUNTRY, AND PARKED OUTSIDE THE HEADQUARTERS OF THE FAA.
SPACEX
HE THEN CALLED A PRESS CONFERENCE.
FALCON
MUSK ANNOUNCED THAT THE FALCON I WAS ONLY THE BEGINNING AND THAT SPACEX WAS ALREADY AT WORK ON A FAR LARGER ROCKET—THE FALCON 5.

AN AMBITIOUS STATEMENT, CONSIDERING THAT SPACEX HAD YET TO LAUNCH EVEN ONE ROCKET.
FALCON
ANY QUESTIONS?
SPACEX HAD BEEN TESTING THE FALCON'S MERLIN AND KESTREL ENGINES AT AN OLD NAVY TEST SITE IN MCGREGOR, TEXAS, WHICH MUSK HAD LEASED.
THE PLAN WAS TO LAUNCH A ROCKET IN EARLY 2004, BUT THAT DATE PASSED AND STILL THERE WAS NO LAUNCH.
IT WAS NOT UNTIL LATE 2004 THAT MUELLER AND HIS TEAM OF ENGINEERS GOT THE ENGINES TO BURN CONSISTENTLY AND SOLVED THE MANY PROBLEMS THAT COME WITH DESIGNING A NEW ROCKET FROM SCRATCH.
THEN THERE WAS ANOTHER SIX-MONTH DELAY AS THE ELECTRONICS FOR THE NAVIGATION, COMMUNICATION, AND OVERALL MANAGEMENT OF THE FALCON WERE FINALIZED.
MUSK'S MANAGERIAL STYLE WAS THE NOW-FAMILIAR MUSK APPROACH OF GRAND, AMBITIOUS STATEMENTS AND UNREALISTIC DEADLINES, AFTER WHICH HE WOULD PUSH HIS WORKFORCE TO PRODUCE MIRACLES.
THIS WHIP IS JUST A METAPHOR, BUT I DO WANT YOU TO WORK HARD.

IN ASHLEE VANCE'S 2015 BOOK, *ELON MUSK: TESLA, SPACEX AND THE QUEST FOR A FANTASTIC FUTURE*, HE QUOTES AN ANONYMOUS ENGINEER.
ELON MUSK
ASHLEE VANCE
MANY GOOD ENGINEERS, ASSETS TO THE COMPANY, EITHER LEFT OR WERE FIRED AFTER BEING BLAMED FOR THINGS THAT WERE NOT THEIR FAULT.
THE KISS OF DEATH WAS PROVING ELON WRONG ABOUT SOMETHING.
SPACEX HAD SPENT $7 MILLION ADAPTING A LAUNCH PAD AT THE VANDENBERG AIR FORCE BASE IN SANTA BARBARA COUNTY, CALIFORNIA.
BUT MANY OF THE TRADITIONAL AEROSPACE COMPANIES, SUCH AS LOCKHEED MARTIN, RESISTED SPACEX USING VANDENBERG. ONE OF THEIR CONCERNS WAS THAT AN UNTRIED ROCKET MIGHT EXPLODE AND DAMAGE THEIR NEARBY FACILITIES.
MUSK AND HIS TEAM LOOKED FOR ANOTHER PLACE AND FOUND KWAJALEIN ISLAND OR KWAJ, THE LARGEST IN AN ATOLL BETWEEN GUAM AND HAWAII IN THE PACIFIC OCEAN.
HOW ABOUT THERE?
AN ISLAND USED BY THE US ARMY AS A MISSILE TEST SITE FOR DECADES.

BY THIS TIME SPACEX HAD GAINED GOVERNMENT BACKING FROM THE DEFENSE ADVANCED RESEARCH PROJECTS AGENCY (DARPA).
DARPA INVESTED A FEW MILLION DOLLARS IN SPACEX. THIS MEANT THAT MUSK WASN'T ENTIRELY CARRYING THE FINANCIAL LOAD ANYMORE.
MARCH 2006, AND AFTER TWO YEARS OF DELAYS, FALCON 1 WAS FINALLY READY TO LIFT OFF.
BUT 25 SECONDS INTO THE LAUNCH...
SPACEX
...THE ROCKET SPUN OUT OF CONTROL...
...AND CRASHED INTO A REEF NOT FAR FROM THE LAUNCHPAD.

DESPITE THIS SETBACK, IN AUGUST 2006, SPACEX RECEIVED GOOD NEWS. THE COMPANY WON A NASA COMMERCIAL ORBITAL TRANSPORTATION SERVICES (COTS) AWARD WORTH UP TO $278 MILLION. THE PROGRAM AIMED AT DEVELOPING PRIVATE COMPANIES TO TAKE OVER THE DELIVERY OF CARGO (AND LATER CREW) TO THE INTERNATIONAL SPACE STATION (ISS).

THE SPACE SHUTTLE PROGRAM WAS DUE TO BE RETIRED IN 2011 AND NASA NEEDED A REPLACEMENT SERVICE. NEVERTHELESS, IT WASN'T UNTIL MARCH 2007 THAT SPACEX ATTEMPTED A SECOND LAUNCH OF THE FALCON 1.

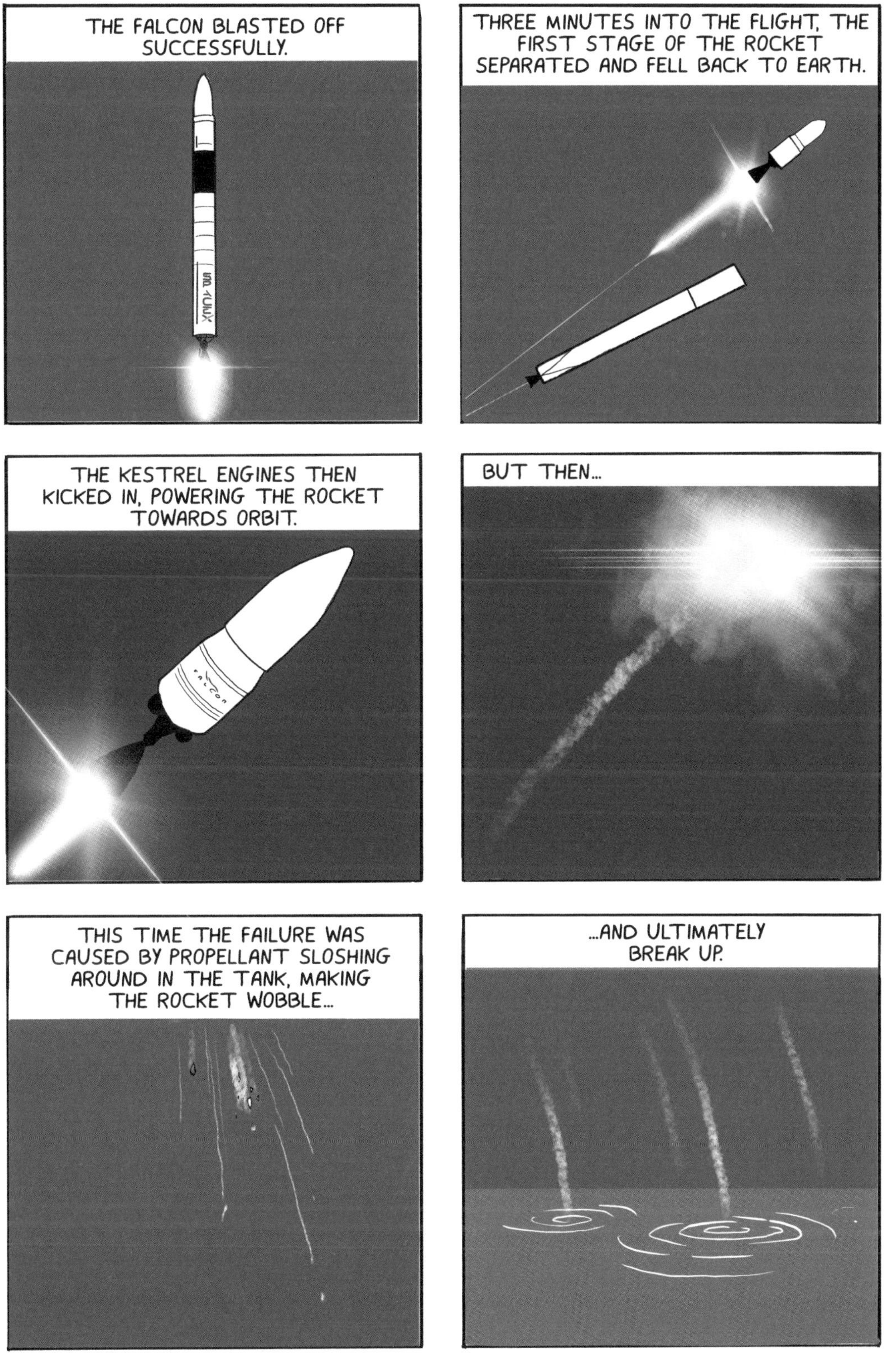
THE FALCON BLASTED OFF SUCCESSFULLY.
THREE MINUTES INTO THE FLIGHT, THE FIRST STAGE OF THE ROCKET SEPARATED AND FELL BACK TO EARTH.
THE KESTREL ENGINES THEN KICKED IN, POWERING THE ROCKET TOWARDS ORBIT.
BUT THEN...
THIS TIME THE FAILURE WAS CAUSED BY PROPELLANT SLOSHING AROUND IN THE TANK, MAKING THE ROCKET WOBBLE...
...AND ULTIMATELY BREAK UP.

THERE WAS A THIRD ATTEMPTED LAUNCH IN AUGUST 2008. THIS TIME THE ROCKET HAD A PAYLOAD: THREE SMALL SATELLITES...
...INCLUDING THE NASA-BUILT MINIATURE LABORATORY PRESAT, A SOLAR SAIL DEMONSTRATOR CALLED NANOSAIL-D, PLUS A PENTAGON SATELLITE CALLED TRAILBLAZER.
THE ROCKET WAS ALSO CARRYING THE ASHES OF 208 PEOPLE WHO HAD PAID TO HAVE THEIR REMAINS FIRED INTO SPACE, INCLUDING *STAR TREK* ACTOR JAMES DOOHAN AND PROJECT MERCURY ASTRONAUT GORDON COOPER.
THE ROCKET FAILED WHEN THE FIRST AND SECOND STAGES COLLIDED WHEN SEPARATING.
SPACEX WAS NOW IN SERIOUS FINANCIAL TROUBLE. MUSK HAD BURNED THROUGH $100 MILLION OF HIS OWN MONEY AND HAD LITTLE MORE TO SPARE.
THE COMPANY COULD AFFORD ONE MORE LAUNCH. IF THAT FAILED, IT WOULD BE THE END OF SPACEX.

MEANWHILE TESLA HAD ENDURED A LONG PERIOD OF PROBLEMS. FIRSTLY, THERE WAS A MAJOR MANUFACTURING ISSUE WITH THE ROADSTER'S TRANSMISSION.
A TRANSMISSION WORKS BY TRANSMITTING THE POWER GENERATED BY THE ENGINE ALONG THE DRIVE SHAFT AND AXLE TO SPIN THE WHEELS.
MULTIPLE VENDORS WERE CONTRACTED TO DESIGN AND BUILD THE MULTI-GEAR TRANSMISSION, BUT NONE OF THE TRANSMISSIONS THESE COMPANIES DELIVERED COULD HANDLE THE INTENSE ROTATIONAL FORCE THE DRIVE SHAFT WAS SUBJECTED TO.
IN THE END, STRAUBEL'S DESIGN TEAM CAME UP WITH THEIR OWN SOLUTION USING A SINGLE-SPEED TRANSMISSION TO ACHIEVE THE HIGH SPEEDS THEY WANTED, BUT NOT BEFORE TESLA HAD WASTED MILLIONS ATTEMPTING TO SOURCE A MULTI-GEAR TRANSMISSION.
THIS MEANT THAT BY THE TIME THE FIRST ROADSTERS WERE ROLLING OFF THE PRODUCTION LINE, THEY WERE ALREADY OBSOLETE.
OBSOLETE
THESE VEHICLES HAD TO BE RETROFITTED WITH A NEW MOTOR, COOLINGSYSTEM, AND SINGLE-SPEED TRANSMISSION. CUSTOMERS WERE ASKED TO PAY MORE FOR CARS THEY'D ALREADY PAID FOR.
MORE.
?

TESLA ALSO HAD PROBLEMS IN ITS BATTERY FACTORY IN THAILAND.
THAILAND
BANGKOK
WHEN TESLA ENGINEERS GOT TO THE SITE, JUST SOUTH OF BANGKOK, THEY FOUND ONLY A CONCRETE SLAB WITH POSTS HOLDING UP A ROOF.
FACTORIES HERE DON'T HAVE WALLS. THEY NEED TO BE OPEN, BECAUSE OF THE FIERCE HEAT.
WELL, AN OPEN FACTORY MIGHT BE FINE FOR MOST MANUFACTURING, BUT OUR SENSITIVE ELECTRONICS NEED TO BE SHIELDED FROM HUMID CONDITIONS.
WALLS HAD TO BE BUILT, THE FLOOR COATED, AND TEMPERATURE-CONTROLLED ROOMS CREATED.
THEN TESLA ENGINEERS HAD TO TRAIN THE THAI WORKERS. THIS CREATED FURTHER DELAYS. ULTIMATELY, THE PLAN TO MANUFACTURE ELECTRONICS IN THAILAND HAD TO BE ABANDONED.

WORSE WAS TO COME. ONE OF TESLA'S INVESTORS, VALOR EQUITY PARTNERS, SENT THEIR MANAGING DIRECTOR OF OPERATIONS, TIM WATKINS, TO AUDIT THE CAR COMPANY.
TESLA
TESLA HOPED TO SELL THE ROADSTER AT A STARTING PRICE OF AROUND $85,000, BUT WATKINS FOUND THAT THE CAR COULD COST AS MUCH AS AN INCREDIBLE $200,000 TO PRODUCE.
THE COST OF EQUIPMENT AND MATERIALS WAS FAR HIGHER THAN ANYONE AT TESLA HAD KEPT TRACK OF. THESE COSTS WOULD BE REDUCED WHEN THE ROADSTER WAS IN FULL PRODUCTION, BUT ONLY DOWN TO $170,000.
WARNING
BANKRUPTCY
IMMINENT
BEFORE THIS DISCOVERY, DISCUSSIONS HAD ALREADY BEGUN ABOUT REPLACING EBERHARD AS CEO, AS EVEN HE ADMITTED THAT TESLA NEEDED SOMEONE WITH MORE MANUFACTURING EXPERIENCE.
WARNING
BANKRUPTCY
IMMINENT
MUSK PUSHED THE IDEA THAT EBERHARD HAD GROSSLY MISMANAGED THE COMPANY AND FAILED TO DISCLOSE THE SOARING COSTS TO THE BOARD.
A DISGRUNTLED EBERHARD WAS THEN DEMOTED TO THE LESSER POSITION OF PRESIDENT OF TECHNOLOGY.
BAH!

THIS LEFT EBERHARD UNHAPPY. HE'D BEEN MOVED OFF ALL MAJOR RESPONSIBILITIES AND SIDELINED INTO DULL TROUBLESHOOTING JOBS.
SO BORED.
EBERHARD WAS A CO-CREATOR OF TESLA. HE'D SEEN THE POTENTIAL OF LITHIUM-ION BATTERIES IN A HIGH-END ELECTRIC SPORTS CAR AND MADE IT A REALITY.
IT WAS MY DREAM.
BUT HE'D ALSO MADE SERIOUS MISTAKES. HE'D UNDERESTIMATED THE SHEER COMPLEXITY OF MAKING A CAR AND HAD ALLOWED THE COMPANY TO LOSE TRACK OF ITS COSTS.
AND WORSE STILL, HE'D LOST CONTROL OF TESLA. BY LATE 2007 ELON MUSK HAD POURED SO MUCH OF HIS OWN MONEY INTO THE CAR COMPANY THAT HE ESSENTIALLY RAN THE BOARD.
MARTIN. I NEED TO SPEAK TO YOU.
MUSK WANTED EBERHARD OUT. SO, ACCORDING TO COURT DOCUMENTS FILED BY EBERHARD, HE MADE HIM AN ULTIMATUM:
SIX MONTHS OF SALARY WORTH $100,000 AND AN OPTION TO PURCHASE 250,000 SHARES IN RETURN FOR HIS EXIT. SIGN NOW OR GET NOTHING.

EBERHARD HAD LITTLE CHOICE BUT TO SIGN.
EXIT
NOT MANY WEEKS AFTER THIS, MARC TARPENNING, THE OTHER COFOUNDER ALSO LEFT, FEELING BURNED OUT AND THAT HE'D DONE AS MUCH AS HE COULD.
UNHAPPY AT THE WAY HE'D BEEN EJECTED FROM HIS OWN COMPANY, EBERHARD BEGAN TO EXPRESS HIS FRUSTRATIONS ONLINE IN HIS TESLA FOUNDERS BLOG...
...WHERE HE DETAILED THE CHANGES TAKING PLACE AT TESLA, COMPLETE WITH QUOTES FROM ANONYMOUS DISGRUNTLED EMPLOYEES.
TOO MANY GOOD PEOPLE HAVE BEEN FIRED TO SAVE COSTS AND IT'S CREATED A BAD ATMOSPHERE.
?
THIS DID NOT GO DOWN WELL AT TESLA. A LAWYER GOT IN TOUCH WITH EBERHARD TO SAY THAT HE'D VIOLATED THE AGREEMENT HE'D SIGNED UPON LEAVING, PART OF WHICH BOUND HIM NOT TO DISPARAGE THE CAR COMPANY.
LEGAL NOTICE
AS A RESULT HIS ABILITY TO VEST IN THE 250,000 STOCK OPTIONS WAS WITHDRAWN.
WE'LL TAKE THIS BACK.

IN A SERIES OF NEWSPAPER AND MAGAZINE STORIES, MUSK BLAMED EBERHARD FOR ALL THAT HAD GONE WRONG AT TESLA.
THEN CAME A FURTHER INSULT. BACK WHEN RELATIONS BETWEEN THE TWO HAD BEEN GOOD, MUSK AND EBERHARD HAD AGREED THAT ELON WOULD GET THE VERY FIRST ROADSTER THAT CAME OFF THE PRODUCTION LINE...
...WHILE EBERHARD WOULD GET THE SECOND, BUT MONTHS PASSED AFTER PRODUCTION BEGAN AND EBERHARD RECEIVED NOTHING.
IN JULY 2008, HE WAS TOLD BY TESLA THAT HIS ROADSTER HAS BEEN DRIVEN INTO THE BACK OF A TRUCK DURING TESTING AND HAD BEEN ALMOST COMPLETELY DESTROYED.
ULTIMATELY, ROADSTER #2 WAS GIVEN TO TESLA BOARD MEMBER ANTONIO GRACIAS.
EBERHARD SUED, CLAIMING LIBEL, SLANDER, AND BREACH OF CONTRACT.
LAWSUIT

EBERHARD'S REPLACEMENT AS TESLA CEO WAS MICHAEL MARKS, WHO'D BEEN THE CEO OF FLEXTRONICS, A HUGE ELECTRONIC MANUFACTURING COMPANY.
MARKS HAD THE EXPERIENCE IN MANUFACTURING AND LOGISTICS THAT TESLA DESPERATELY NEEDED.
THIS COMPANY HAS A LOT OF ISSUES.
MARKS' VIEW OF EBERHARD WAS MORE POSITIVE THAN MUSK'S. HE'S QUOTED IN TIM HIGGINS' BOOK ON TESLA, AS SAYING THAT ALTHOUGH HE BELIEVED THAT IT WAS RIGHT TO REMOVE EBERHARD AS CEO...
POWER PLAY
TIM HIGGINS
...HE DIDN'T BELIEVE THAT EBERHARD HAD LIED TO THE BOARD. MARKS ALSO STATED THAT EVEN AFTER EBERHARD HAD BEEN REMOVED FROM HIS POST HE'D REMAINED COMMITTED AND ENTHUSIASTIC ABOUT TESLA, AND THAT SHOULD BE PART OF HIS RECORD.
HE DID EVERYTHING I ASKED.
THE DISPUTE BETWEEN MUSK AND EBERHARD WAS ULTIMATELY SETTLED OUT OF COURT.
THE TERMS WERE CONFIDENTIAL, BUT IT IS KNOWN THAT THERE WAS A NON-DISPARAGEMENT AGREEMENT. AND THAT EBERHARD GOT HIS SHARES BACK.
AND A ROADSTER.

MICHAEL MARKS DID NOT LAST LONG AS TESLA CEO. HE AND MUSK HAD VERY DIFFERENT IDEAS ABOUT THE FUTURE OF THE COMPANY.
TESLA'S ONLY PRODUCT HAD MISSED NUMEROUS DEADLINES AND THE COMPANY WAS HEMORRHAGING MONEY. INVESTORS WERE NERVOUS.
?
?
THERE WERE ONLY TWO OPTIONS AS FAR AS MARKS COULD SEE: EITHER FIND A PARTNER TO HELP COSTS (CHRYSLER WAS LATER BRIEFLY COURTED), OR SELL TESLA OUTRIGHT.
PARTNER
SELL
THESE PLANS DID NOT GO DOWN WELL WITH MUSK, WHO DID NOT WANT TO LOSE CONTROL OF THE COMPANY. HE SHOWED MARKS THE DOOR.
IT'S OVER THERE.
OUT
MARKS' REPLACEMENT WAS ZE'EV DRORI, AN ISRAEL-BORN AMERICAN WHO'D BEEN THE FOUNDER AND CHIEF EXECUTIVE OF MONOLITHIC MEMORIES, A COMPUTER MEMORY COMPANY BEFORE IT HAD BEEN SOLD TO ADVANCED MICRO DEVICES.
HI!
BUT DRORI LASTED LESS THAN A YEAR IN THE JOB BEFORE SWITCHING TO THE POSITION OF TESLA'S VICE-CHAIRMAN. MUSK HIMSELF THEN BECAME CEO.

THE FOURTH ATTEMPT TO LAUNCH FALCON I TOOK PLACE ON SEPTEMBER 28, 2008.
MUSK HAD POURED $100 MILLION INTO SPACEX, BUT BECAUSE OF THE PROBLEMS AT TESLA HE HAD NO SPARE MONEY TO TRY AGAIN. IF THIS FLIGHT DIDN'T SUCCEED, IT WAS THE END.
BUT IT DID SUCCEED. AFTER SIX YEARS, SPACEX PUT A ROCKET IN ORBIT.
MUSK WAS ECSTATIC.
THERE ARE A LOT OF PEOPLE WHO THOUGHT WE COULDN'T DO IT.
THERE ARE ONLY A HANDFUL OF COUNTRIES ON EARTH THAT HAVE DONE THIS. IT'S NORMALLY A COUNTRY THING, NOT A COMPANY THING.
MY MIND IS KIND OF FRAZZLED, SO IT'S HARD FOR ME TO SAY ANYTHING, BUT MAN, THIS IS DEFINITELY ONE OF THE GREATEST DAYS IN MY LIFE.

DESPITE THIS ACHIEVEMENT, BOTH OF MUSK'S COMPANIES WERE IN SERIOUS TROUBLE.
FINANCIAL WOES
THE GENERAL OPINION IN THE MEDIA WAS THAT TESLA WAS DOOMED. A WEBSITE CALLED THE TRUTH ABOUT CARS BEGAN A TESLA "DEATH WATCH," PUBLISHING DOZENS OF NEGATIVE ARTICLES ABOUT THE CAR COMPANY.
TESLA
THEN A SILICON VALLEY GOSSIP AND NEWS SITE CALLED *VALLEYWAG* PUBLISHED AN EMAIL FROM A TESLA WHISTLEBLOWER STATING THAT...
TESLA MOTORS
THE COMPANY HAS JUST GONE THROUGH A ROUND OF LAYOFFS, SHUT DOWN ITS DETROIT OFFICE, AND HAS ONLY $9 MILLION LEFT IN THE BANK.
TESLA HAS TAKEN 1,200 ROADSTER PREORDERS FROM CUSTOMERS, RAKING IN TENS OF MILLIONS OF DOLLARS, BUT HAS ONLY DELIVERED FIFTY CARS.
ON TOP OF THIS FINANCIAL PRESSURE, MUSK WAS ALSO GOING THROUGH A VERY PUBLIC DIVORCE.
GOSSIP
INSIDE ELON MUSK'S

IN LATE 2008 TESLA PUT OUT A PRESS RELEASE ANNOUNCING A $40 MILLION FINANCING COMMITMENT, ESSENTIALLY LOANS FROM INVESTORS TO BE REPAID IN SHARES AT SOME POINT IN THE FUTURE.
TECH NEWS
TESLA SAVED
BUT THE TRUTH WAS THAT THE DEAL HADN'T BEEN FINALIZED YET AND WOULDN'T BE FOR AMOST TWO MORE MONTHS.
TECH NEWS
TESLA SAVED
MUSK HAD TO BORROW CASH FROM SPACEX AND LIQUIDATE ASSETS TO TRY AND GET THE $20 MILLION HE NEEDED INVESTORS TO MATCH. IN THE END, HE ONLY MANAGED TO SCRAPE TOGETHER $12 MILLION.
TWO DAYS BEFORE CHRISTMAS, SPACEX GOT THE GIFT OF A $1.6 BILLION CONTRACT FOR UP TO TWELVE FLIGHTS TO DELIVER CARGO TO THE INTERNATIONAL SPACE STATION FROM NASA.
THANK YOU, SANTA.
THANK THE US TAXPAYERS. IT'S THEIR MONEY.
CONTRACT
THE TESLA DEAL WAS FINALLY SIGNED BY INVESTORS ONLY DAYS BEFORE THE COMPANY WOULD HAVE GONE BANKRUPT. MUSK THREATENED TO FUND THE ENTIRE $40 MILLION HIMSELF, USING MORE MONEY BORROWED FROM THE NEWLY SOLVENT SPACEX.
YOU CAN SAY GOODBYE TO THOSE FUTURE SHARES IF YOU DON'T SIGN.
OKAY. WE'LL SIGN.

THIS WOULD NOT BE THE LAST TIME A MUSK COMPANY RECEIVED TAXPAYER MONEY.
MORE.
IN 2007, WHEN EBERHARD WAS CEO OF TESLA, THE COMPANY HAD APPLIED TO THE US GOVERNMENT FOR A $350 MILLION LOAN TO DEVELOP AN ELECTRIC SEDAN, CODE NAME "WHITESTAR."
AND ANOTHER $100 MILLION TO DEVELOP A BATTERY PRODUCTION FACILITY THAT COULD SUPPLY OTHER ELECTRIC CAR MAKERS.
THIS MONEY WOULD COME OUT OF THE $25 BILLION FUND CREATED BY THE ENERGY INDEPENDENCE AND SECURITY ACT TO SUPPORT ADVANCED TECHNOLOGY VEHICLES.
THE ACT WAS SIGNED INTO LAW BY PRESIDENT GEORGE W. BUSH IN DECEMBER 2007, AS PART OF HIS ATTEMPT TO REDUCE AMERICAN DEPENDENCY ON GASOLINE.
HOWEVER, IN ORDER TO QUALIFY FOR THIS MONEY, TESLA HAD TO PROVE TO THE GOVERNMENT THAT IT WASN'T A LOSS-MAKING COMPANY.
WELL, HOW DO WE KNOW TESLA ISN'T GOING TO GO BANKRUPT?

TESLA HAD TO ACHIEVE PROFITABLY AND THIS INEVITABLY MEANT SQUEEZING THE CUSTOMERS AGAIN, EVEN THOSE WHO HAD PAID IN ADVANCE.
MUSK DIDN'T RAISE PRICES ON THE CARS THIS TIME. INSTEAD, CUSTOMERS FOUND THEY WOULD HAVE TO PAY EXTRA FOR PREVIOUSLY INCLUDED OPTIONS...
TESLA MOTORS
...SUCH AS A 240-VOLT CHARGER THAT COULD CHARGE A ROADSTER IN EIGHT HOURS, WITHOUT WHICH A BASIC-VERSION BUYER WOULD BE STUCK WITH A 120-VOLT CHARGER THAT COULD TAKE THIRTY-PLUS HOURS TO CHARGE.
HOW LONG WILL IT TAKE TO CHARGE?
THE PRICE TAG FOR THESE OPTIONS—THAT CUSTOMERS ALREADY THOUGHT THEY'D BOUGHT—WAS $6,700 TO $9,350.
MAYBE TUESDAY.
MUSK GAMBLED THAT THERE WOULD BE FEW CANCELLATIONS, AS MOST ROADSTER CUSTOMERS WERE WEALTHY ENOUGH TO BE ABLE TO AFFORD THE INCREASES, AND IN THIS HE WAS PROVED CORRECT.
IT WAS STILL A CRUMMY MOVE ON TESLA'S PART.
IN EARLY AUGUST 2009, TESLA ANNOUNCED THE COMPANY HAD ACHIEVED ITS FIRST-EVER PROFITABLE MONTH, WITH $1 MILLION IN PROFIT AND $20 MILLION IN REVENUE.

BUT THE TRUTH WAS THAT TESLA DIDN'T GAIN THIS PROFITABILITY ENTIRELY THROUGH SELLING ELECTRIC CARS. MOST OF THE COMPANY'S PROFIT THAT YEAR TO DATE HAD COME FROM SELLING ZEV CREDITS.
Z
WHAT ARE ZEV CREDITS? ZEV STANDS FOR "ZERO EMISSION VEHICLE." THE ZEV PROGRAM IS A STATE LAW THAT APPLIES IN CALIFORNIA, COLORADO, CONNECTICUT, MAINE, MARYLAND, MASSACHUSETTS, NEW JERSEY, NEW YORK, OREGON, RHODE ISLAND, VERMONT, AND WASHINGTON.
TO PUT IT SIMPLY, THE ZEV PROGRAM'S OBJECTIVE IS TO ENCOURAGE CAR MAKERS TO RESEARCH, DEVELOP, AND MARKET ELECTRIC VEHICLES, AS THESE CARS GENERATE LESS POLLUTION AND FEWER GLOBAL WARMING EMISSIONS THAN GAS-POWERED CARS.
IT'S A LITTLE MORE COMPLICATED THAN CAR COMPANIES EARNING ZEV CREDITS FOR EACH ELECTRIC VEHICLE SOLD, BUT THAT IS ESSENTIALLY WHAT HAPPENS.
CARS COMPANIES CAN EITHER BANK OR SELL THEIR ZEV CREDITS TO OTHER AUTOMOBILE MANUFACTURERS.
...AND SELL ZEV CREDITS IS WHAT TESLA DID IN ORDER TO PUSH IT OVER THE LINE TO MAKE ITS QUARTERLY PROFIT IN AUGUST 2009.
WE DID IT.

ONE MILLION DOLLARS IS BARELY A PROFIT WHEN YOU CONSIDER THE MORE THAN $200 MILLION THAT INVESTORS HAD PUMPED INTO TESLA, BUT IT WAS SUFFICIENT FOR THE COMPANY TO RECEIVE THE $465 MILLION GOVERNMENT LOAN IT WANTED, AN AMOUNT LARGER THAN ALL THE PREVIOUS FUNDING ROUNDS COMBINED.
BIG GOVERNMENT
$
FINANCIAL WOES RESOLVED, TESLA BEGAN DEVELOPMENT OF ITS MODEL S SEDAN.
WHILE STILL A LUXURY SEDAN, THE MODEL S WAS TESLA'S FIRST STEP AWAY FROM HIGH-END SPORTS CAR DRIVERS AND TOWARDS MAINSTREAM CONSUMERS.
THE MAN MUSK HIRED TO DESIGN THE MODEL S WAS FRANZ VON HOLZHAUSEN.
BORN IN CONNECTICUT, HOLZHAUSEN BEGAN HIS CAREER WITH VOLKSWAGEN, WHERE HE WORKED ON THE DESIGNS FOR THE MICROBUS AND THE NEW BEETLE.

FROM THERE HE'D MOVED ON TO GENERAL MOTORS AS A DESIGN MANAGER AND THEN TO MAZDA AS CHIEF OF DESIGN.
GM
MAZDA
HOLZHAUSEN HAD BECOME TIRED OF THE SLUGGISH CORPORATE CULTURE OF BIG AUTO FIRMS. WITH TESLA, HE FELT HE HAD A CHANCE TO CREATE SOMETHING GENUINELY INNOVATIVE.
HEY, YOU CAN'T DO THAT.
THEN I'M LEAVING.
HE PROBABLY HAD NO IDEA WHEN HE LEFT HIS SECURE JOB AT MAZDA JUST HOW CLOSE TESLA HAD COME TO BANKRUPTCY.
TESLA
WHAT HOLZHAUSEN DESIGNED, WITH MUCH INPUT FROM MUSK, WAS A SLEEK SEDAN THAT EVOKED THE CONTOURS OF AN ASTON MARTIN, BUT WITH SUCH A LARGE INTERIOR SPACE...
...THAT TESLA CLAIMED A MOUNTAIN BIKE, A SURFBOARD, AND A FIFTY-INCH TV COULD LIE FLAT INSIDE AT THE SAME TIME.
THIS SPACE WAS ACHIEVED BY PLACING THE BATTERIES IN A BOX BENEATH THE FLOOR WHILE THE MOTOR, FAR SMALLER THAN A GAS-POWERED ENGINE, SAT BETWEEN THE BACK WHEELS.

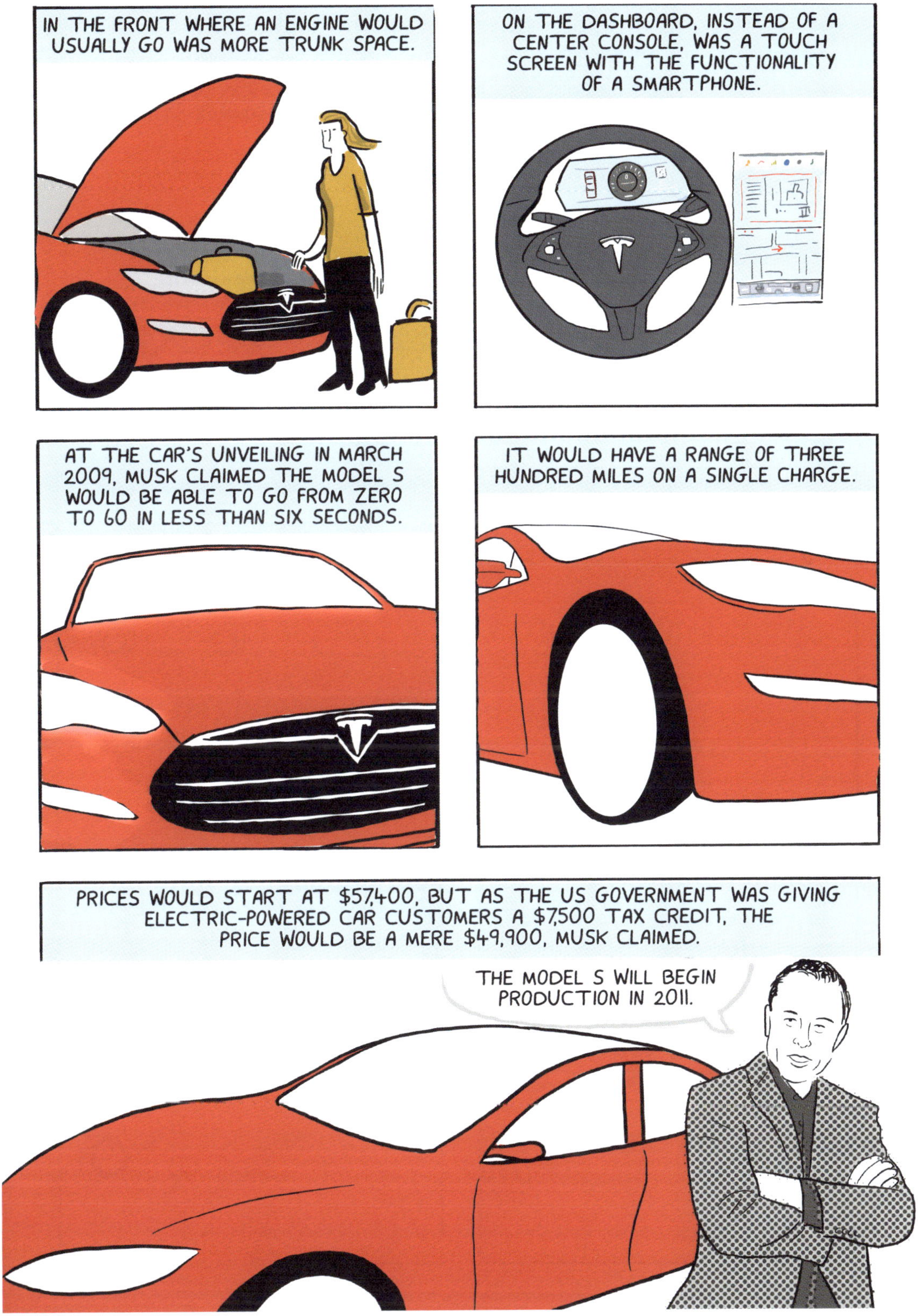
IN THE FRONT WHERE AN ENGINE WOULD USUALLY GO WAS MORE TRUNK SPACE.
ON THE DASHBOARD, INSTEAD OF A CENTER CONSOLE, WAS A TOUCH SCREEN WITH THE FUNCTIONALITY OF A SMARTPHONE.
AT THE CAR'S UNVEILING IN MARCH 2009, MUSK CLAIMED THE MODEL S WOULD BE ABLE TO GO FROM ZERO TO 60 IN LESS THAN SIX SECONDS.
IT WOULD HAVE A RANGE OF THREE HUNDRED MILES ON A SINGLE CHARGE.
PRICES WOULD START AT $57,400, BUT AS THE US GOVERNMENT WAS GIVING ELECTRIC-POWERED CAR CUSTOMERS A $7,500 TAX CREDIT, THE PRICE WOULD BE A MERE $49,900, MUSK CLAIMED.
THE MODEL S WILL BEGIN PRODUCTION IN 2011.

QUESTIONS AS TO WHERE THE MODEL S WAS TO BE BUILT WERE ANSWERED IN MAY 2010 WHEN TESLA ANNOUNCED THAT IT WOULD BE PURCHASING AN AUTOMOBILE MANUFACTURING PLANT IN FREMONT, CALIFORNIA, FROM TOYOTA FOR $42 MILLION. AS PART OF THE DEAL, TOYOTA WOULD ALSO BUY $50 MILLION OF COMMON STOCK WHEN TESLA WENT PUBLIC THE FOLLOWING MONTH.

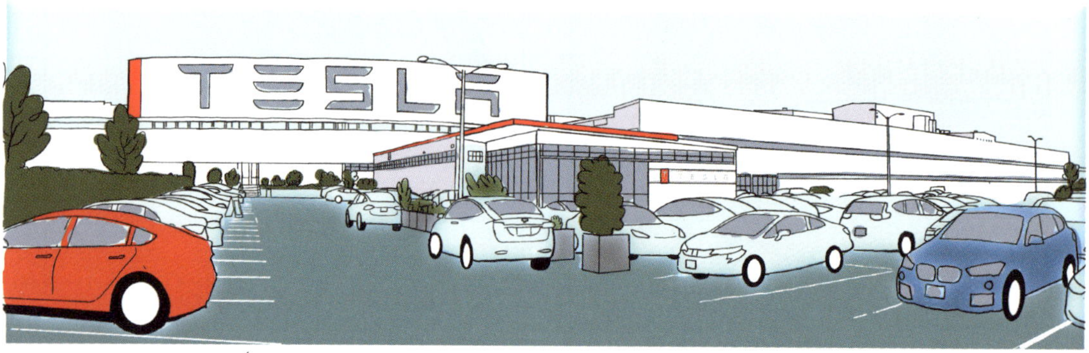

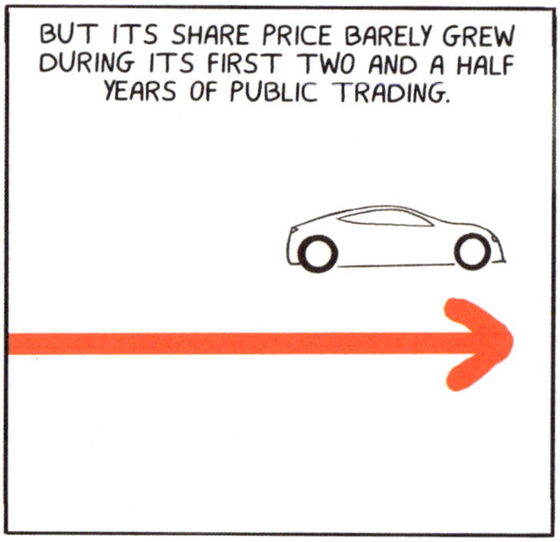

SINCE 2008, MUSK HAD BEEN DATING ENGLISH ACTRESS TALULAH RILEY.
RILEY'S FILM WORK INCLUDED PRIDE AND PREJUDICE (2005), ST TRINIAN'S (2007), THE BOAT THAT ROCKED (2009), AND INCEPTION (2010). HER TV WORK INCLUDED POIROT, NEARLY FAMOUS, AND DR. WHO.
THEY'D MET IN A LONDON CLUB, WHISKY MIST, IN MAYFAIR. HE'D SHOWED HER PHOTOS OF THE FALCON I AND THE ROADSTER ON HIS PHONE.
SHE DIDN'T REALISE MUSK OWNED THE COMPANIES THAT BUILT THESE MACHINES.
I THOUGHT HE'D JUST DONE SOME WORK ON THEM.
MUSK PROPOSED AFTER KNOWING HER ONLY A COUPLE OF WEEKS.
THEY WERE MARRIED IN 2010 AT DORNOCH CATHEDRAL IN SCOTLAND.

IN APRIL THAT YEAR, PRESIDENT OBAMA ENDORSED SPACEX WHEN HE WAS GIVEN A TOUR BY MUSK AROUND THE COMPANY'S COMPLEX AT THE KENNEDY SPACE CENTER IN CAPE CANAVERAL, FLORIDA.
SPACEX
TWO MONTHS LATER, SPACEX'S FALCON 9, A REUSABLE HEAVIER-LIFT VEHICLE, LAUNCHED FROM THE SPACE CENTER AND ORBITED THE EARTH SUCCESSFULLY.
IN DECEMBER 2010 THE FALCON 9 CARRIED AN UNMANNED "DRAGON" CAPSULE INTO SPACE. THIS CAPSULE WAS THEN SUCCESSFULLY RECOVERED FROM THE OCEAN.
THE BELL-SHAPED DRAGON CAPSULE HAD BEEN SPECIFICALLY DESIGNED TO CARRY ASTRONAUTS OR CARGO TO THE INTERNATIONAL SPACE STATION.
A SECOND DRAGON TEST FLIGHT SUCCESSFULLY DOCKED WITH THE INTERNATIONAL SPACE STATION IN MAY 2012, DELIVERING CARGO.
THIS ACHIEVEMENT PROMPTED NASA TO GIVE SPACEX $440 MILLION TO FURTHER DEVELOP THE DRAGON CAPSULE.
NICE.

IN SEPTEMBER 2011 AT A SPEECH AT THE NATIONAL PRESS CLUB IN WASHINGTON, D.C., MUSK ANNOUNCED PLANS FOR SPACEX TO BUILD THE WORLD'S FIRST COMPLETELY REUSABLE ROCKET.
A FULLY REUSABLE ROCKET WILL DRAMATICALLY DECREASE THE COST OF SENDING CARGO AND HUMANS TO SPACE, MAKING THE EXPLORATION AND COLONIZATION OF OTHER WORLDS, SUCH AS MARS, MORE FEASIBLE.
IN THE SPACEX PLAN EACH OF THE TWO STAGES OF THE ROCKET WOULD BE REUSABLE.
SPACEX
THE STAGES WOULD NOT GLIDE BACK ON WINGS LIKE THE SPACE SHUTTLE. THEY WOULD INSTEAD DESCEND VERTICALLY…
SPACEX
…EVENTUALLY SETTLING DOWN ON FOUR LEGS.
THEY COULD THEN BE REFUELED AND RELAUNCHED.

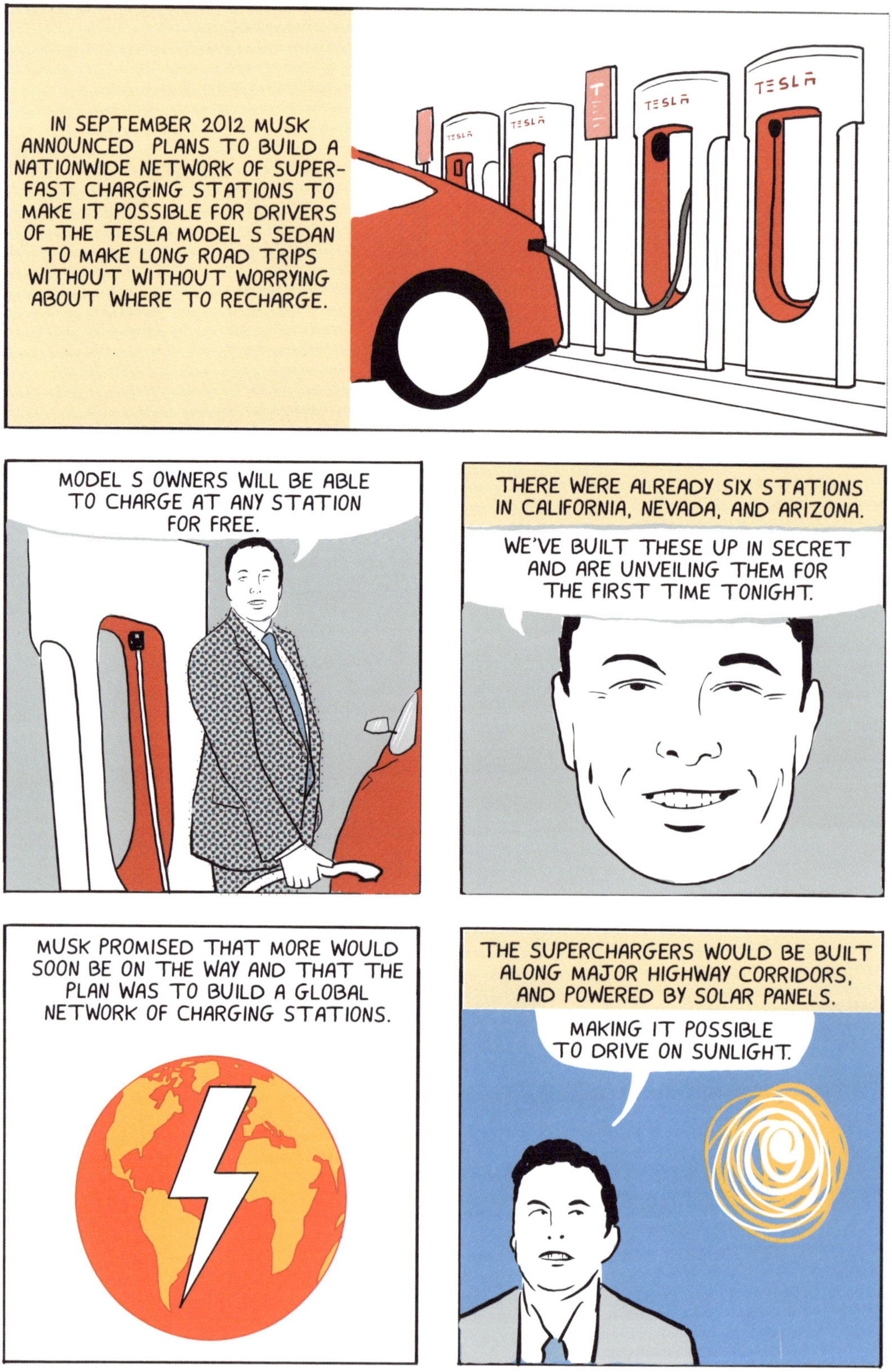
IN SEPTEMBER 2012 MUSK ANNOUNCED PLANS TO BUILD A NATIONWIDE NETWORK OF SUPER-FAST CHARGING STATIONS TO MAKE IT POSSIBLE FOR DRIVERS OF THE TESLA MODEL S SEDAN TO MAKE LONG ROAD TRIPS WITHOUT WITHOUT WORRYING ABOUT WHERE TO RECHARGE.
MODEL S OWNERS WILL BE ABLE TO CHARGE AT ANY STATION FOR FREE.
THERE WERE ALREADY SIX STATIONS IN CALIFORNIA, NEVADA, AND ARIZONA.
WE'VE BUILT THESE UP IN SECRET AND ARE UNVEILING THEM FOR THE FIRST TIME TONIGHT.
MUSK PROMISED THAT MORE WOULD SOON BE ON THE WAY AND THAT THE PLAN WAS TO BUILD A GLOBAL NETWORK OF CHARGING STATIONS.
THE SUPERCHARGERS WOULD BE BUILT ALONG MAJOR HIGHWAY CORRIDORS, AND POWERED BY SOLAR PANELS.
MAKING IT POSSIBLE TO DRIVE ON SUNLIGHT.

THE SOLAR PANELS WOULD BE SUPPLED BY SOLARCITY, A COMPANY STARTED BY MUSK'S COUSINS PETER AND LYNDON RIVE. MUSK HAD INVESTED IN SOLARCITY AND WAS THE CHAIRMAN.
TESLA WOULD EVENTUALLY BUY SOLARCITY FOR $2.6 BILLION AND INCORPORATE THE COMPANY INTO ITS OWN BUSINESS.
THE "POWERED BY THE SUN" CLAIM HAS YET TO HAPPEN. TESLA DOES HAVE SOLAR POWER AT SOME SUPER-CHARGER STATIONS, BUT MOST CHARGING STATIONS ARE STILL POWERED BY THE GRID. NOR IS CHARGING FREE.
I KNEW IT WAS TOO GOOD TO BE TRUE.
DESPITE MUSK'S BEST ATTEMPTS TO HYPE THE COMPANY, AT THE END OF 2012, SALES OF THE MODEL S WERE AT BEST SLUGGISH. THAT YEAR TESLA LOST NEARLY $400 MILLION.
IT COULD ENDURE THESE LOSSES ONLY THROUGH THE DEPARTMENT OF ENERGY GOVERNMENT LOAN, INVESTMENTS FROM DAIMLER, TOYOTA, AND PANASONIC, PLUS MONEY GENERATED FROM ITS LAUNCH ON THE STOCK MARKET.
AND THE MONEY WAS STILL RUNNING OUT.
TESLA DID FINALLY MANAGE TO DELIVER THE FIRST MODEL S IN THE SUMMER OF 2012, A YEAR LATE, BUT PRODUCTION WAS ACHINGLY SLOW.
COME ON!
TESLA

BUT THEN A MIRACLE HAPPENED. PRODUCTION AND SALES OF THE MODEL S BEGAN TO PICK UP. BY MARCH 2013 TESLA RECORDED AN $11 MILLION PROFIT FOR THE FIRST QUARTER OF THAT YEAR.
TESLA
HOW DID TESLA ACHIEVE THIS? IT SEEMED TO BE A COMBINATION OF FIRING UNDERPERFORMING SALES EXECUTIVES, FOCUSING MORE ON WHAT CUSTOMERS WANTED...
RED WAS POPULAR, SO RED WAS 40 PERCENT OF PRODUCTION FOR AT LEAST THREE MONTHS.
...ENDING THE REFUNDABLE RESERVATION PAYMENT AND TURNING IT INTO AN ACTUAL DEPOSIT FOR THE CAR. RAVE REVIEWS FOR THE MODEL S APPEARED IN AUTOMOBILE MAGAZINES. BUT ONCE AGAIN CAR SALES WERE NOT THE ONLY STORY. ZEV CREDITS WERE ALSO A BIG PART OF TESLA'S PROFITABILITY.
CAR STUFF
TESLA MADE ABOUT 10 PERCENT OF ITS INCOME—$40.5 MILLION—FROM SELLING EMISSIONS CREDITS TO OTHER AUTOMAKERS.
THIS IS WAS WHEN TESLA'S STOCK BEGAN ZOOMING UPWARD.

BY THE END OF 2013, WHEN MUSK WAS NAMED *FORTUNE'S* BUSINESSPERSON OF THE YEAR, THE VALUE OF HIS SHARE OF TESLA WAS WORTH MORE THAN $5.5 BILLION.
FORTUNE
2013
#1
ELON MUSK
IT COULD SO EASILY HAVE GONE DIFFERENTLY. JUST PRIOR TO THE UPTURN IN TESLA'S FORTUNES, MUSK HAD MADE A TENTATIVE APPROACH TO GOOGLE, OFFERING TO SELL HIS COMPANY TO THE TECH GIANT FOR AROUND $6 BILLION.
HOW ABOUT IT?
AS PART OF THIS DEAL MUSK WOULD HAVE REMAINED CEO OF TESLA FOR EIGHT YEARS, OR UNTIL THE FIRST MASS-MARKET ELECTRIC CAR WAS PRODUCED.
CAN WE BE FRIENDS?
SPECIFICS OF THE SALE WERE STILL BEING WORKED OUT WHEN TESLA BEGAN TO TURN A PROFIT AND MUSK SUDDENLY DIDN'T NEED GOOGLE.
OH, FORGET IT.
MUSK THEN PAID OFF TESLA'S GOVERNMENT DEBT YEARS EARLY, WITH $12 MILLION IN INTEREST.
THANKS.
BIG GOVERNMENT
$

PERHAPS NOT SURPRISINGLY MUSK'S PERSONAL LIFE SUFFERED DURING THE ENDLESS PRESSURE OF RUNNING TWO MAJOR BUSINESSES. RILEY FILED FOR DIVORCE IN 2012.
BUT THE COUPLE REMARRIED IN 2013.
THE MARRIAGE LASTED ANOTHER THREE YEARS. THEY DIVORCED AGAIN IN 2016.
RILEY CONTINUED WITH HER ACTING CAREER, APPEARING IN TWO SEASONS OF HBO'S *WESTWORLD*, AMONG OTHER ROLES.
MUSK HAS REMAINED ON FRIENDLY TERMS WITH RILEY.
HE'S THE PERFECT EX-HUSBAND.
MEANWHILE, TESLA WAS DEVELOPING ITS MODEL X.

UNVEILED IN 2012, THE MODEL X WAS TESLA'S THIRD PRODUCTION VEHICLE AND IS CONSIDERED THE WORLD'S FIRST MODERN PRODUCTION ALL-ELECTRIC SUV.

THE CAR'S MOST STRIKING FEATURE WAS THE FALCON-WING DOORS THAT OPENED UPWARDS INSTEAD OF OUTWARDS.

TESLA CLAIMED THAT THE MODEL X WOULD BE ABLE TO DRIVE 250 MILES PER CHARGE AND HIT 60 MPH FROM A STANDING START IN 3.2 SECONDS WITH A TOP SPEED OF 155 MPH.

IT CAME WITH A WHOLE RANGE OF SENSORS INCLUDING CAMERAS, RADAR AND SONAR SYSTEMS WHICH ENABLED PARTIAL SELF-DRIVING AND AUTOMATIC BRAKING SAFETY FEATURES.

THE PLAN WAS FOR TESLA TO BEGIN DELIVERIES IN EARLY 2014, BUT THAT DATE CAME AND WENT WITHOUT ANY CUSTOMER GETTING THEIR CAR.

STATED REASONS FOR THE DELAYS WERE PROBLEMS WITH THE FALCON-WING DOORS AND ISSUES COOLING THE ELECTRIC MOTORS WHEN THE CAR HAULED TRAILERS.
WHERE IS IT?

TESLA WAS EVENTUALLY TO FILE A LAWSUIT AGAINST SWISS HYDRAULICS FIRM HOERBIGER HOLDING. TESLA CLAIMED THE DOORS SUFFERED FROM OIL LEAKAGE AND OVERHEATING. THE LAWSUIT WAS SETTLE IN MEDIATION FOR UNDISCLOSED TERMS.
IN THE END, TESLA RESOLVED THE DOOR PROBLEM BY DESIGNING A LESS COMPLICATED ELECTROMECHANICAL SYSTEM, BUILDING THEM IN-HOUSE.
DELIVERIES OF THE MODEL X DIDN'T BEGIN UNTIL SEPTEMBER 2015—MORE THAN A YEAR AFTER ORIGINALLY SCHEDULED.
FINALLY.
I'M KEEN TO TRY OUT THE MANY HIGH-TECH FEATURES THIS CAR HAS INSTALLED, WHICH MUSK CLAIMS ARE THE BASIS UPON WHICH TESLAS WILL BE SELF-DRIVING IN THE FUTURE.
ACCORDING TO EDWARD NIEDERMEYER IN HIS BOOK *LUDICROUS: THE UNVARNISHED STORY OF TESLA MOTORS*, MUSK DIDN'T SHOW ANY REAL INTEREST IN SELF-DRIVING CARS UNTIL AFTER HIS ATTEMPTED SALE OF TESLA TO GOOGLE.

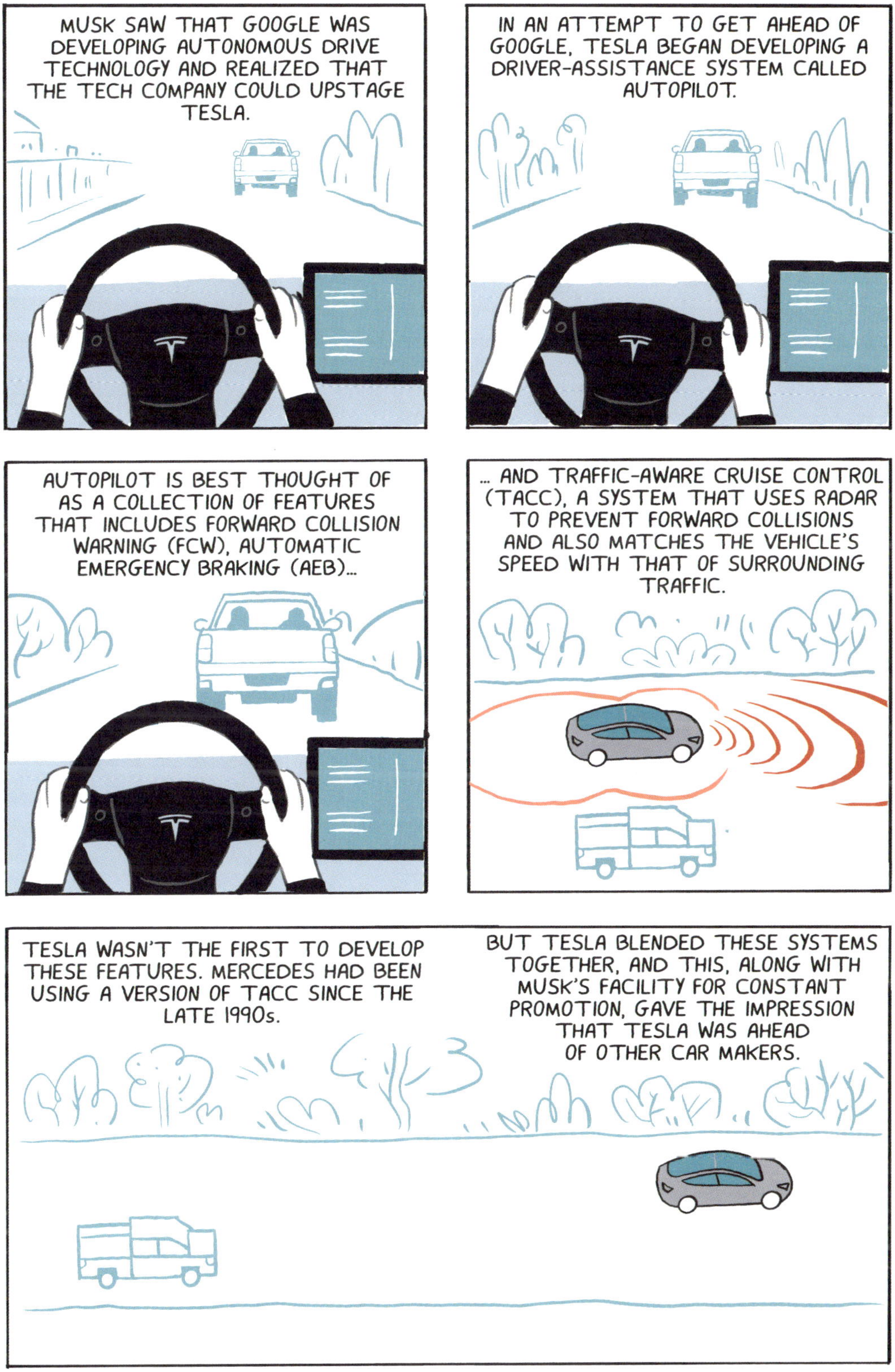
MUSK SAW THAT GOOGLE WAS DEVELOPING AUTONOMOUS DRIVE TECHNOLOGY AND REALIZED THAT THE TECH COMPANY COULD UPSTAGE TESLA.
IN AN ATTEMPT TO GET AHEAD OF GOOGLE, TESLA BEGAN DEVELOPING A DRIVER-ASSISTANCE SYSTEM CALLED AUTOPILOT.
AUTOPILOT IS BEST THOUGHT OF AS A COLLECTION OF FEATURES THAT INCLUDES FORWARD COLLISION WARNING (FCW), AUTOMATIC EMERGENCY BRAKING (AEB)...
... AND TRAFFIC-AWARE CRUISE CONTROL (TACC), A SYSTEM THAT USES RADAR TO PREVENT FORWARD COLLISIONS AND ALSO MATCHES THE VEHICLE'S SPEED WITH THAT OF SURROUNDING TRAFFIC.
TESLA WASN'T THE FIRST TO DEVELOP THESE FEATURES. MERCEDES HAD BEEN USING A VERSION OF TACC SINCE THE LATE 1990s.
BUT TESLA BLENDED THESE SYSTEMS TOGETHER, AND THIS, ALONG WITH MUSK'S FACILITY FOR CONSTANT PROMOTION, GAVE THE IMPRESSION THAT TESLA WAS AHEAD OF OTHER CAR MAKERS.

TESLA BEGAN FITTING THE AUTOPILOT HARDWARE INTO THEIR CARS IN 2014, BUT THE SYSTEM DIDN'T BECOME FULLY FUNCTIONAL UNTIL AN ONLINE SOFTWARE UPDATE IN 2015.
THE MOST CONTROVERSIAL ASPECT OF AUTOPILOT IS AUTOSTEER, A SYSTEM WHICH KEEPS THE VEHICLE WITHIN LANE MARKINGS WITHOUT DRIVER INPUT.
IN THEORY THIS COULD ALLOW THE DRIVER TO TAKE HIS OR HER HANDS OFF THE STEERING WHEEL. SOMETHING THAT TESLA DID NOT ADVISE.
STOP
TESLA EMPHASIZED THAT AUTOPILOT REQUIRED CONSTANT DRIVER ATTENTION AND THAT THE SOFTWARE WAS ONLY THERE AS AN ASSIST.
IN HIS ENTHUSIASM FOR THE NEW TECHNOLOGY, MUSK HAD NOT ALWAYS MADE THAT CLEAR, BUT THE OFFICIAL COMPANY LINE WAS THAT NO TESLA CAR COULD SELF-DRIVE YET.
MEANWHILE, AT MUSK'S OTHER COMPANY, A GENUINE TECHNOLOGICAL BREAKTHROUGH HAD TAKEN PLACE.
SPACEX

IN MCGREGOR, TEXAS, SPACEX HAD BEEN TESTING THE GRASSHOPPER, ITS REUSABLE VERTICAL-TAKEOFF-AND-LANDING ROCKET.
THE FIRST TEST FLIGHT OF THE ROCKET TOOK PLACE IN SEPTEMBER 2012, WHEN GRASSHOPPER MADE A QUICK SIX-FOOT JUMP UP AND DOWN.
OVER THE FOLLOWING YEAR, THE ROCKET DEMONSTRATED AN ABILITY TO FIGHT BACK AGAINST WIND GUSTS, AS WELL AS TO MOVE SIDEWAYS THROUGH THE AIR TO ITS TARGET LANDING POINT.
GRASSHOPPER MADE EIGHT TEST FLIGHTS. THE FINAL TEST FLIGHT WAS ON OCTOBER 7, 2013, FLYING TO AN ALTITUDE OF 744 METERS BEFORE MAKING A SUCCESSFUL LANDING.
WE'VE PROVEN IT WORKS. NOW IT'S TIME TO MOVE ONTO BIGGER THINGS.
SPACEX THEN BEGAN USING THEIR FALCON 9 VEHICLES FOR REUSABLE VERTICAL-TAKEOFF-AND-LANDING TESTING. NUMEROUS OVER-WATER LANDINGS WERE ATTEMPTED, SOME ONTO BARGES MODIFIED INTO LANDING PLATFORMS.
AT FIRST WITHOUT SUCCESS.

WITH EACH FAILURE MORE WAS LEARNED, SO THAT GRADUALLY SPACEX EDGED CLOSER TO SUCCESS.
DECEMBER 21, 2015, SAW THE FIRST VERTICAL LANDING OF A FALCON 9 ROCKET.

IN AUGUST 2013, MUSK UNVEILED A CONCEPT FOR A HIGH-SPEED TRANSPORTATION SYSTEM CALLED HYPERLOOP. PASSENGERS WOULD TRAVEL IN PODS, WHICH WOULD RIDE ON AIR CUSHIONS DRIVEN BY MAGNETIC LEVITATION AND AIR COMPRESSORS, ALL ENCLOSED INSIDE LOW-PRESSURE TUBES.

IN HIS 57-PAGE WHITE PAPER, WRITTEN WITH DESIGN ASSISTANCE FROM A GROUP OF ENGINEERS FROM BOTH TESLA MOTORS AND SPACEX, MUSK POINTED OUT THAT IN OTHER MODES OF TRANSPORT, A SIGNIFICANT AMOUNT OF ENERGY IS LOST OVERCOMING FRICTION AND WIND RESISTANCE, BUT THE LOW PRESSURE INSIDE THE TUBES OF THE HYPERLOOP WOULD REDUCE THESE OBSTACLES TO ALMOST NOTHING. THESE PODS WOULD BE ABLE TO MOVE AT EXTREMELY HIGH SPEEDS ON LOW HORSE-POWER. MUSK PROPOSED LINKING LOS ANGELES AND SAN FRANCISCO. PASSENGERS WOULD TRAVEL THE ROUGHLY 350 MILES BETWEEN THE TWO CITIES IN 35 MINUTES AT A TOP SPEED OF 760 MPH.

MUSK WOULD LATER ADMIT THAT HIS MOTIVATION FOR PUSHING THE HYPERLINK CONCEPT WAS HIS HATRED FOR CALIFORNIA'S PROPOSED HIGH-SPEED RAIL SYSTEM, WHICH HE THOUGHT WAS NOT NEARLY AMBITIOUS ENOUGH. HE HOPED THE HYPERLINK IDEA WOULD PROVOKE LEGISLATORS INTO CONSIDERING MORE INSPIRED AND CREATIVE SOLUTIONS.

MUSK HAD NO INTENTION OF BUILDING HYPERLOOP, BUT SPACEX DID SPONSOR A HYPERLOOP POD DESIGN COMPETITION TO HELP PROMOTE THE TECHNOLOGY.
THIS ANNUAL EVENT TOOK PLACE ON A TEST TRACK NEAR SPACEX'S HEADQUARTERS, FROM 2015 TO 2019.
THE COMPETITION WAS OPEN TO STUDENT TEAMS AND HOBBYISTS FROM ACROSS THE GLOBE. AT THE TIME OF THE LAST COMPETITION IN 2019 THE TEST TRACK HAD REACHED ONE MILE.
IN 2022 THE TRACK WAS TORN DOWN AND REPLACED WITH A PARKLING LOT FOR SPACEX EMPLOYEES.
IN THE END, IT SEEMS THAT HYPERLOOP WAS A BILLIONAIRE'S WHIM, A THOUGHT EXPERIMENT MUSK HOPED OTHERS WOULD TAKE UP.
A PROJECT HE HAD LITTLE TIME FOR WHEN HE HAD BOTH TESLA AND SPACEX TO RUN.

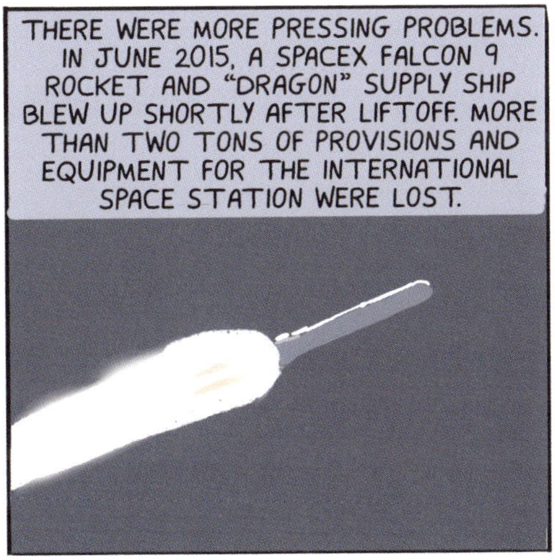
THERE WERE MORE PRESSING PROBLEMS. IN JUNE 2015, A SPACEX FALCON 9 ROCKET AND "DRAGON" SUPPLY SHIP BLEW UP SHORTLY AFTER LIFTOFF. MORE THAN TWO TONS OF PROVISIONS AND EQUIPMENT FOR THE INTERNATIONAL SPACE STATION WERE LOST.

THE CAUSE OF THE EXPLOSION WAS THE RUPTURE OF THE FALCON 9'S UPPER-STAGE LIQUID OXYGEN TANK, TRIGGERED BY A PRESSURIZED HELIUM VESSEL THAT BROKE FREE IN FLIGHT.

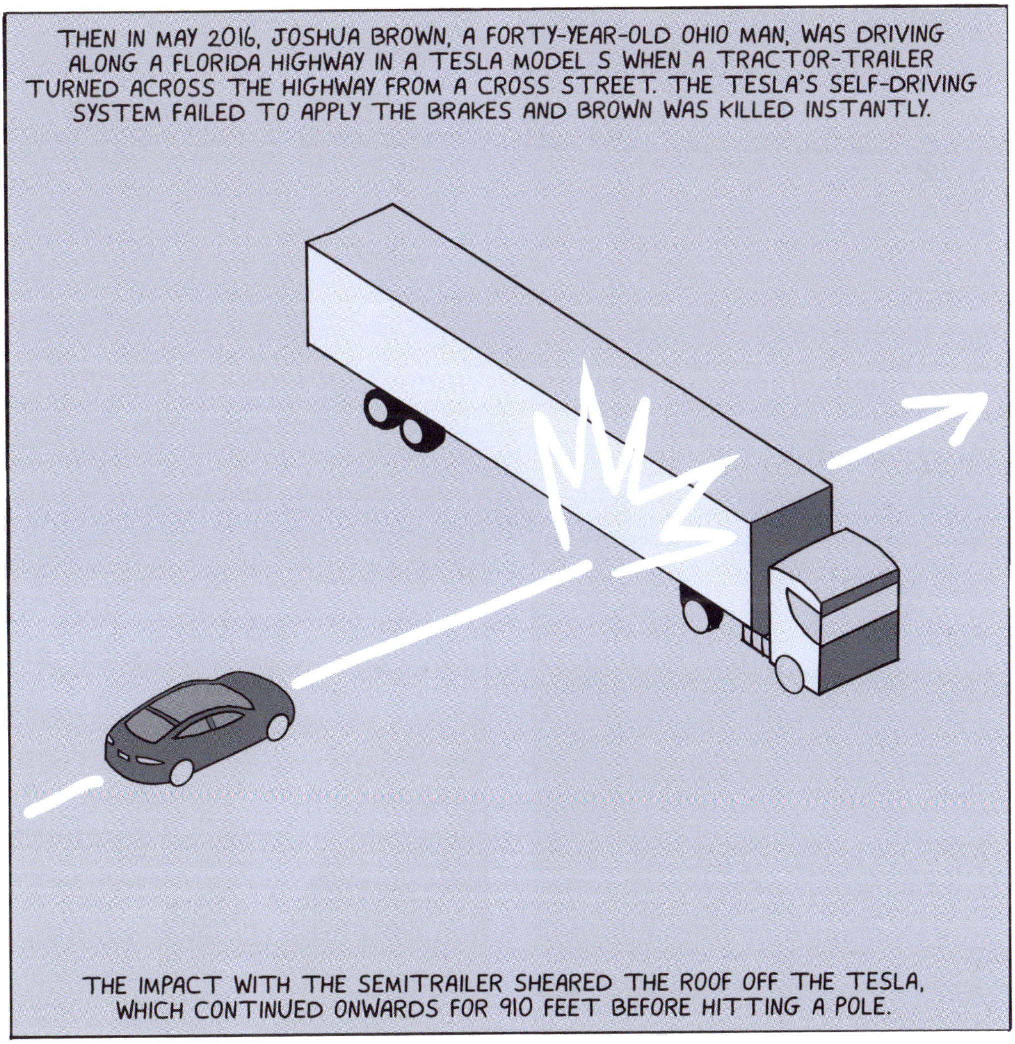
THEN IN MAY 2016, JOSHUA BROWN, A FORTY-YEAR-OLD OHIO MAN, WAS DRIVING ALONG A FLORIDA HIGHWAY IN A TESLA MODEL S WHEN A TRACTOR-TRAILER TURNED ACROSS THE HIGHWAY FROM A CROSS STREET. THE TESLA'S SELF-DRIVING SYSTEM FAILED TO APPLY THE BRAKES AND BROWN WAS KILLED INSTANTLY.
THE IMPACT WITH THE SEMITRAILER SHEARED THE ROOF OFF THE TESLA, WHICH CONTINUED ONWARDS FOR 910 FEET BEFORE HITTING A POLE.

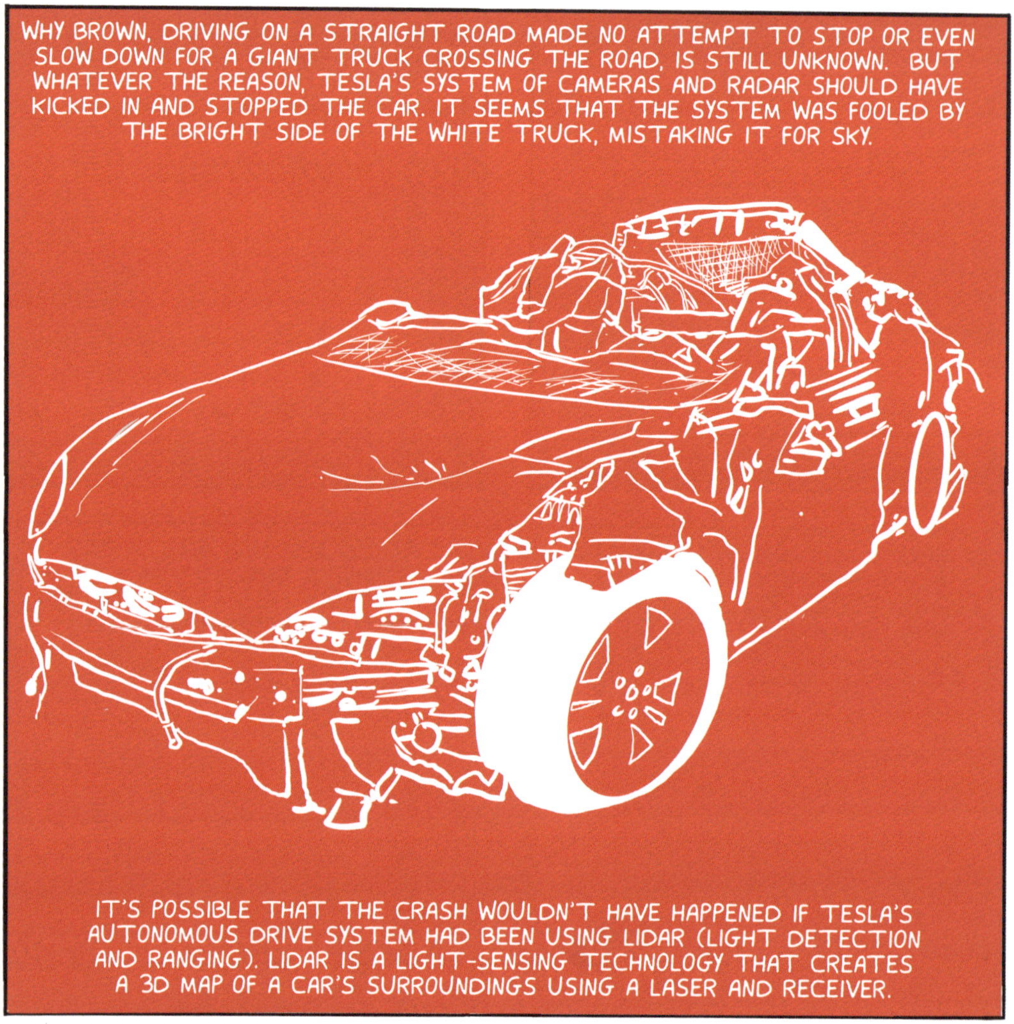
WHY BROWN, DRIVING ON A STRAIGHT ROAD MADE NO ATTEMPT TO STOP OR EVEN SLOW DOWN FOR A GIANT TRUCK CROSSING THE ROAD, IS STILL UNKNOWN. BUT WHATEVER THE REASON, TESLA'S SYSTEM OF CAMERAS AND RADAR SHOULD HAVE KICKED IN AND STOPPED THE CAR. IT SEEMS THAT THE SYSTEM WAS FOOLED BY THE BRIGHT SIDE OF THE WHITE TRUCK, MISTAKING IT FOR SKY.
IT'S POSSIBLE THAT THE CRASH WOULDN'T HAVE HAPPENED IF TESLA'S AUTONOMOUS DRIVE SYSTEM HAD BEEN USING LIDAR (LIGHT DETECTION AND RANGING). LIDAR IS A LIGHT-SENSING TECHNOLOGY THAT CREATES A 3D MAP OF A CAR'S SURROUNDINGS USING A LASER AND RECEIVER.

MUSK HAD MADE A DECISION NOT TO USE THIS TECHNOLOGY IN ORDER TO REDUCE BOTH COST AND SOFTWARE COMPLEXITY, EVEN THOUGH OTHER CAR MAKERS WERE USING LIDAR.

MUSK AT TESLA'S AUTONOMY INVESTOR DAY, APRIL 2019.
LIDAR IS A FOOL'S ERRAND. ANYONE RELYING ON LIDAR IS DOOMED. DOOMED! (THEY ARE) EXPENSIVE SENSORS THAT ARE UNNECESSARY.
T

LESS THAN THREE MONTHS AFTER THE CRASH THAT KILLED JOSHUA BROWN, AUTOMOTIVE SAFETY EQUIPMENT COMPANY MOBILEYE TERMINATED ITS RELATIONSHIP WITH TESLA.
CON
TRACT
MOBILEYE PROVIDED TESLA WITH THE COMPUTER CHIPS AND PROGRAMMING IN THE CAMERA-BASED SEMI-AUTONOMOUS DRIVING SYSTEM USED IN THE MODEL S AND MODEL X.
MOBILEYE CEO AMNON SHASHUA LATER REVEALED HE WAS WORRIED THAT TESLA WAS PUSHING THE TECHNOLOGY BEYOND SAFE CAPABILITIES.
HE TOLD REUTERS THAT AUTOPILOT WAS NOT A DRIVERLESS SYSTEM, BUT A DRIVER-ASSISTANCE SYSTEM.
TESLA FIRED BACK THAT COMMERCIAL CONCERNS CAUSED THE SPLIT, SAYING THAT MOBILEYE WAS ANGRY THAT TESLA WAS DEVELOPING A VIDEO-PROCESSING SYSTEM OF ITS OWN.
DAN GALVES, MOBILEYE'S CHIEF COMMUNICATIONS OFFICER, REPLIED THAT THE REASONS FOR THE BREAKUP WERE EXACTLY THOSE SHASHUA STATED, IN ADDITION TO COMMERCIAL ISSUES THAT WERE NOT FOR PUBLIC DISCUSSION.

IN THE END, TESLA WAS EXONERATED IN THE NATIONAL HIGHWAY TRAFFIC SAFETY ADMINISTRATION'S INVESTIGATION. THE NHTSA NOT ONLY CONCLUDED THAT AUTOPILOT SHOULD NOT BE RECALLED, BUT CLAIMED THAT STATISTICS SHOWED TESLA'S CRASH RATES HAD DROPPED BY 40 PERCENT AFTER "AUTOSTEER" WAS INSTALLED.
SHERIFF

NOT EVERYBODY WAS CONVINCED. A SMALL RESEARCH AND CONSULTING FIRM CALLED QUALITY CONTROL SYSTEMS (QCS) FILED A FREEDOM OF INFORMATION ACT REQUEST IN PURSUIT OF DATA THAT THE NATIONAL HIGHWAY TRAFFIC SAFETY ADMINISTRATION HAD WITHHELD FROM PUBLIC VIEW.

WHAT QCS DISCOVERED WAS THAT THE MAJORITY OF THE VEHICLES IN THE TESLA DATA SET WERE MISSING DATA AND THAT THIS MISSING DATA MADE IT IMPOSSIBLE TO CONCLUDE WHETHER AUTOSTEER INCREASED OR DECREASED THE CRASH RATE. OF THE 5,714 VEHICLES WHOSE DATA WASN'T MISSING, QCS FOUND THAT AUTOSTEER WAS ACTUALLY ASSOCIATED WITH AN INCREASED CRASH RATE OF 59 PERCENT.

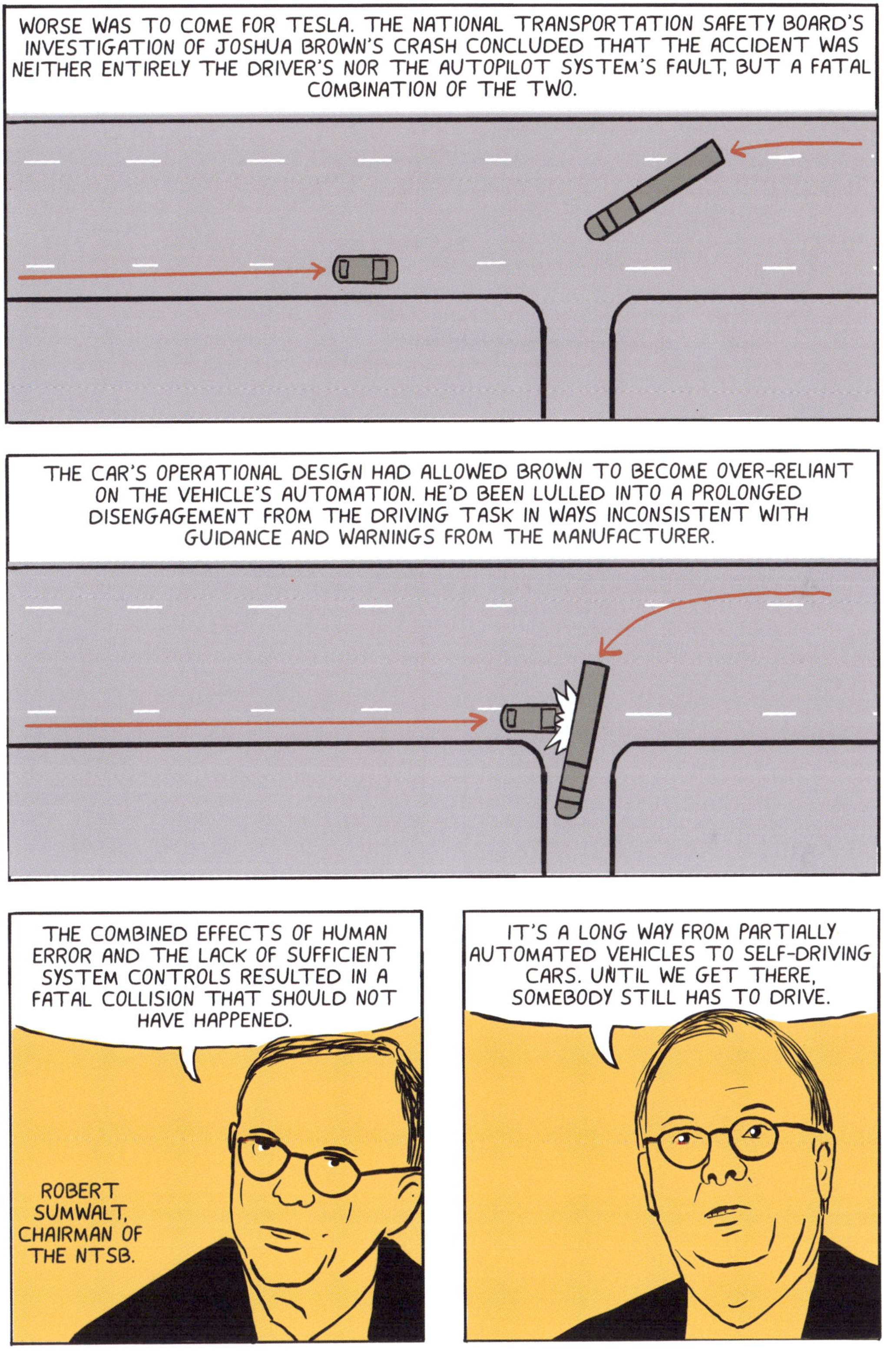
WORSE WAS TO COME FOR TESLA. THE NATIONAL TRANSPORTATION SAFETY BOARD'S INVESTIGATION OF JOSHUA BROWN'S CRASH CONCLUDED THAT THE ACCIDENT WAS NEITHER ENTIRELY THE DRIVER'S NOR THE AUTOPILOT SYSTEM'S FAULT, BUT A FATAL COMBINATION OF THE TWO.
THE CAR'S OPERATIONAL DESIGN HAD ALLOWED BROWN TO BECOME OVER-RELIANT ON THE VEHICLE'S AUTOMATION. HE'D BEEN LULLED INTO A PROLONGED DISENGAGEMENT FROM THE DRIVING TASK IN WAYS INCONSISTENT WITH GUIDANCE AND WARNINGS FROM THE MANUFACTURER.
THE COMBINED EFFECTS OF HUMAN ERROR AND THE LACK OF SUFFICIENT SYSTEM CONTROLS RESULTED IN A FATAL COLLISION THAT SHOULD NOT HAVE HAPPENED.
ROBERT SUMWALT, CHAIRMAN OF THE NTSB.
IT'S A LONG WAY FROM PARTIALLY AUTOMATED VEHICLES TO SELF-DRIVING CARS. UNTIL WE GET THERE, SOMEBODY STILL HAS TO DRIVE.

TESLA RESPONDED TO THE CRASH BY UPDATING THE AUTOPILOT SOFTWARE SO THAT IF THE DRIVER DIDN'T TAKE THE WHEEL AFTER THREE WARNINGS, THE CAR WOULD SLOW TO A STOP.
WHY HAVE WE STOPPED?
THE CAR GOT ANNOYED WITH ME.
THE COMPANY LINE REMAINED THAT TESLA'S CARS WEREN'T SELF-DRIVING AND THAT DRIVERS SHOULD ALWAYS BE ATTENTIVE AND HAVE THEIR HANDS ON THE WHEEL.
I HAVE FAITH IN MUSK. HE'S A TECH GENIUS. I'M SURE SELF-DRIVING CARS WILL BE ALONG ANY MINUTE.
BUT MUSK'S TENDENCY TO MAKE WILD PREDICTIONS, WHICH WERE THEN HYPED UP BY UNCRITICAL MEDIA, OFTEN BLURRED THE COMPANY MESSAGE.
TESLAS ARE MORE OR LESS SELF-DRIVING NOW, AREN'T THEY?
IN OCTOBER 2016, ONLY FIVE MONTHS AFTER JOSHUA BROWN'S DEATH, MUSK SAID IN A PRESS CALL THAT...
A TESLA VEHICLE WILL DRIVE IN FULLY AUTONOMOUS MODE FROM L.A. TO NEW YORK CITY BY THE END OF 2017.
FULLY AUTONOMOUS VEHICLES STILL HAVE NOT ARRIVED AT THE TIME OF WRITING IN 2025, AND THERE IS NO SIGN THAT ANY ARE IMMINENT.
SIGH!

MORE WILD CLAIMS WERE MADE BY MUSK IN 2016 WHEN HE AND A GROUP OF SCIENTISTS AND ENGINEERS FOUNDED NEURALINK.
NEURALINK IS A COMPANY THAT AIMS TO DEVELOP BRAIN-COMPUTER INTERFACES THAT CONNECT THE HUMAN BRAIN TO A COMPUTER.
MUSK INVESTED TENS OF MILLIONS OF HIS OWN WEALTH INTO THE COMPANY. HE CLAIMED THAT NEURALINK'S DEVICES WOULD ENABLE PARALYZED PEOPLE TO OPERATE ROBOTIC LIMBS AND WOULD CURE DEAFNESS, BLINDNESS, AND OTHER DISABILITIES.
THE TECHNOLOGY WOULD ALLOW ME TO CONTROL THIS ROBOTIC ARM WITH MY MIND, FOR EXAMPLE.
THERE HAD BEEN A SMALL AMOUNT OF PROGRESS BY 2021. THE COMPANY RELEASED A VIDEO SHOWING A MACAQUE PLAYING THE VIDEO GAME PONG USING A NEURALINK BRAIN IMPLANT.
THE PHYSICIANS COMMITTEE FOR RESPONSIBLE MEDICINE, A MEDICAL RESEARCH NONPROFIT, HAS BEEN HIGHLY CRITICAL OF NEURALINK'S TREATMENT OF MONKEYS.
THEY DRILLED INTO MY BRAIN.
THE GROUP SUED THE UNIVERSITY OF CALIFORNIA DAVIS PRIMATE RESEARCH CENTER, WHICH HAD PARTNERED WITH NEURALINK, FOR THE RELEASE OF RECORDS DETAILING EXPERIMENTS CONDUCTED ON MONKEYS.
BRAIN-CONTROL OF COMPUTER CURSORS BY MONKEYS IS NOT EVEN NEW. A GROUP OF RESEARCHERS DEMONSTRATED THIS BACK 2002.

THE RELEASED PAGES SHOWED THAT ANIMALS SUFFERED FROM POOR QUALITY EXPERIMENTS, RESULTING IN CHRONIC INFECTIONS, SEIZURES, PARALYSIS, INTERNAL BLEEDING, AND DECLINING PSYCHOLOGICAL HEALTH BEFORE THEY WERE EUTHANIZED.
AN UNAPPROVED ADHESIVE WAS USED IN TWO INCIDENTS TO FILL HOLES IN MONKEYS' SKULLS.
THE ADHESIVE CAUSED BLEEDING IN ONE MONKEY'S BRAIN, CAUSING SO MUCH VOMITING THAT SHE DEVELOPED OPEN SORES IN HER ESOPHAGUS.
IN DECEMBER 2022 REUTERS REPORTED THAT A FEDERAL PROBE HAD BEEN OPENED BY THE US DEPARTMENT OF AGRICULTURE, FOCUSING ON VIOLATIONS OF THE ANIMAL WELFARE ACT BY NEURALINK.

REUTERS ALSO REPORTED THERE WAS GROWING EMPLOYEE DISSENT WITHIN THE COMPANY ABOUT NEURALINK'S ANIMAL TESTING. PRESSURE FROM MUSK, IT WAS CLAIMED, HAD PUSHED EMPLOYEES TO ACCELERATE DEVELOPMENT, SO THAT UNDER-PREPARED AND OVER-STRESSED STAFF RUSHED TO MEET DEADLINES, CREATING RISKS TO THE ANIMALS.
I'M LEAVING BECAUSE OF MY CONCERNS OVER ANIMAL TESTING.
EXIT

IN 2022, THE US FOOD AND DRUG ADMINISTRATION (FDA) REJECTED NEURALINK'S APPLICATION TO PURSUE HUMAN CLINICAL TRIALS DUE TO...
...CONCERNS INVOLVING THE DEVICE'S LITHIUM BATTERY...
...THE POTENTIAL FOR THE IMPLANT'S THINNER-THAN-A-HUMAN-HAIR WIRES TO MIGRATE TO OTHER AREAS OF THE BRAIN...
...AND QUESTIONS OVER WHETHER AND HOW THE DEVICE COULD BE REMOVED WITHOUT DAMAGING BRAIN TISSUE.
NEURALINK WAS EVENTUALLY GIVEN THE GO-AHEAD TO BEGIN HUMAN TRIALS IN 2023.
NEURALINK'S MAIN COMPETITOR IN THE FIELD IS SYNCHRON, WHICH AIMS TO HELP PARALYZED PEOPLE TYPE WITH THEIR MINDS. THE TECHNOLOGY SYNCHRON USES DOESN'T INVOLVE SURGERY ON THE SKULL.
INSTEAD ITS DEVICE IS INSERTED THROUGH A BLOOD VESSEL. SYNCHRON RECEIVED FDA CLEARANCE FOR HUMAN TRIALS IN 2021.

YET ANOTHER ELON MUSK ENTERPRISE IS STARLINK. TECHNICALLY A DIVISION OF SPACEX, STARLINK IS THE NAME OF THE SPACEFLIGHT COMPANY'S GROWING NETWORK OF SATELLITES. STARLINK INTENDS TO PROVIDE SATELLITE INTERNET ACCESS COVERAGE TO OVER ONE HUNDRED COUNTRIES, WITH THE EVENTUAL AIM OF CREATING A GLOBAL MOBILE PHONE SERVICE.
DEVELOPMENT OF THE STARLINK CONSTELLATION OF SATELLITES BEGAN IN 2015. THE FIRST TWO PROTOTYPE SATELLITES WERE LAUNCHED IN FEBRUARY 2018. SPACEX HAS SINCE MADE OVER TWO HUNDRED SUCCESSFUL LAUNCHES AND DEPLOYED THOUSANDS OF STARLINK SATELLITES INTO LOW EARTH ORBIT.

SPACEX EVENTUALLY HOPES TO HAVE AS MANY AS 42,000 SATELLITES IN A MEGA CONSTELLATION.

THE COMPANY CLAIMS THAT STARLINK IS IDEALLY SUITED FOR AREAS WHERE CONNECTIVITY HAS BEEN UNRELIABLE OR COMPLETELY UNAVAILABLE.

SPACEX PLANS TO REFRESH THE STARLINK MEGA CONSTELLATION EVERY FIVE YEARS. OLDER SATELLITES WILL BE GUIDED INTO EARTH'S ATMOSPHERE TO BURN UP.
CRITICISMS OF STARLINK HAVE COME FROM THE EUROPEAN SPACE AGENCY (ESA) AND THE UNIVERSITY OF SOUTHAMPTON'S ASTRONAUTICS RESEARCH GROUP (ARS) WHO ARE CONCERNED THAT SUCH A LARGE NUMBER OF SATELLITES WILL LEAD TO ORBITAL COLLISIONS ON A REGULAR BASIS.
THERE ARE ALSO WORRIES THAT BURNING THOUSANDS OF SATELLITES IN THE UPPER ATMOSPHERE COULD ALTER THE ATMOSPHERIC CHEMISTRY WITH UNFORESEEN CONSEQUENCES FOR LIFE ON THE EARTH.
IN A PAPER PUBLISHED IN THE JOURNAL *SCIENTIFIC REPORTS* IN MAY 2021, CANADIAN RESEARCHER AARON BOLEY EXPLAINED THAT...
WHEN BURNED, THE ALUMINUM THE SATELLITES ARE MADE OF WILL PRODUCE ALUMINUM OXIDE, ALSO KNOWN AS ALUMINA.
ALUMINA IS KNOWN TO CAUSE OZONE DEPLETION THAT ALTERS THE ATMOSPHERE'S ABILITY TO REFLECT HEAT.
ONCE LAUNCHED, STRINGS OF STARLINK SATELLITES CAN EASILY BE SEEN BY THE NAKED EYE.

THE BRIGHTENING OF THE NIGHT SKY BY STARLINK SATELLITES HAS ALSO BEEN A POINT OF CONTROVERSY FOR ASTRONOMERS...
...WHO ARE CONCERNED THAT SUCH A MASS OF LOW-ORBIT OBJECTS WILL IMPEDE ASTRONOMICAL OBSERVATIONS.
IT'S JUST TOO BRIGHT.
STARLINK HAS ATTEMPTED TO FIX THE BRIGHTNESS PROBLEM. IN 2020, THE COMPANY TESTED A "DARKSAT" SATELLITE WITH A NON-REFLECTIVE COATING, BUT THIS RESULTED IN OVERHEATING ISSUES.
I'M TOO HOT.
IN JUNE 2020, THE COMPANY LAUNCHED A "VISORSAT" SATELLITE WITH A SUNSHADE VISOR. SINCE THEN ALL STARLINK SATELLITES HAVE BEEN EQUIPPED WITH VISORS.
NOW I'M COOL.
MEASUREMENTS OF THE VISORSAT SHOW SPACEX HAS SUCCEEDED IN MAKING A LESS REFLECTIVE SATELLITE. BUT THEY ARE STILL VISIBLE FROM DARK-SKY AREAS.
OF COURSE, THE SPACE VISORS DON'T LOOK LIKE THIS. I'VE BEEN DRAWN THIS WAY FOR HUMOROUS EFFECT.
I COMMEND THEM FOR THEIR EFFORT. NOW, IF STARLINK COULD JUST AVOID BURNING UP THEIR JUNK IN THE UPPER ATMOSPHERE, BECAUSE THAT MAKES AS MUCH ECOLOGICAL SENSE AS DUMPING TONS OF PLASTIC IN THE OCEANS.

IN 2016 MUSK FOUNDED THE BORING COMPANY WITH THE AIM OF BUILDING A NETWORK OF UNDERGROUND TUNNELS TO TRANSPORT PEOPLE AND CARGO AROUND CITIES.
THE INITIAL IDEA WAS THAT TESLAS WOULD DRIVE FROM THE STREET ONTO ELEVATOR PLATFORMS CALLED CAR "SKATES" AND THEN LOWERED TO TUNNELS BELOW GROUND...
...AND BE PROPELLED AT 120 TO 150 MILES PER HOUR TO THEIR DESTINATIONS.
HOWEVER, WHEN THE BORING COMPANY DEBUTED THEIR TEST TUNNEL UNDER SPACEX PROPERTY AT THE END OF 2018, WHAT WAS REVEALED WAS JUST A REGULAR TESLA DRIVING THROUGH A BUMPY PAVED TUNNEL...
...REACHING A MAXIMUM OF ONLY 40 MILES AN HOUR. IT WAS NOT EVEN SELF-DRIVING.
THIS DID NOT STOP PEOPLE FROM BEING VERY EXCITED ABOUT THE CONCEPT. CITIES LARGE AND SMALL EXPRESSED INTEREST IN HAVING TUNNELS BUILT.
THIS COULD SOLVE OUR INFRASTRUCTURE PROBLEMS.

CITIES IN CALIFORNIA, KENTUCKY, TEXAS, FLORIDA, AND ELSEWHERE EXPRESSED INTEREST IN BUILDING TUNNELS FOR CARS.
WE MUST HAVE TUNNELS.
MUSK CLAIMED HIS COMPANY COULD IMPROVE TUNNELING SPEEDS WITH FULLY ELECTRIFIED MACHINES AND BY DIGGING CONTINUOUSLY WITHOUT STOPPING TO ASSEMBLE SECTIONS OF THE TUNNEL WALL.
TUNNEL INDUSTRY EXPERTS POINTED OUT THAT TUNNEL-BORING MACHINES HAVE BEEN ELECTRIFIED FOR DECADES AND CONTINUOUS CONSTRUCTION OF TUNNEL LINING WASN'T NEW EITHER.
SOUNDS LIKE A RICH GUY'S VANITY PROJECT.
THIS CRITICISM DIDN'T STOP INVESTORS JUMPING IN WITH $675 MILLION IN SERIES C FUNDING THAT PUSHED THE VALUE OF THE COMPANY TO $5.675 BILLION IN APRIL 2022.
$
TO DATE, THE BORING COMPANY'S ONLY OPERATIONAL TUNNEL IS INSIDE THE LAS VEGAS CONVENTION CENTER...
...WHERE HUMAN-DRIVEN TESLAS MOVE AT A SPEED OF AROUND 35 MILES AN HOUR THROUGH THE 1.7-MILE, $47 MILLION TUNNEL.
TESLA

MEANWHILE, TESLA SURGED ON. PRODUCTION OF THE MODEL 3, A FOUR-DOOR SEDAN, BEGAN IN JULY 2017.
PRODUCTION WAS PLAGUED BY THE NOW-ROUTINE TESLA MANUFACTURING DIFFICULTIES. THIS SEEMS TO HAVE LED DOUG FIELD, SENIOR VICE PRESIDENT OF ENGINEERING, TO LEAVE THE COMPANY...
...AFTER MUSK REPORTEDLY PUSHED HIM ASIDE AND TOOK OVER MODEL 3 PRODUCTION HIMSELF.
TIM HIGGINS' BOOK ON TESLA, *POWER PLAY: TESLA, ELON MUSK, AND THE BET OF THE CENTURY*, RELATES STORIES OF MUSK IN THIS PERIOD SCREAMING AT EMPLOYEES IN MEETINGS AND FIRING WHOMEVER HE CAME ACROSS ON THE FACTORY FLOOR...
GET THIS DONE OR GET OUT.
...AS HE ATTEMPTED TO PUSH HIS WORKFORCE TO MEET IMPOSSIBLE AND UNREALISTIC DEADLINES.
WAIT, DIDN'T I FIRE YOU YESTERDAY?
MUSK FELT SO ILL WITH THE PRESSURE THAT ON THE DAY TESLA ANNOUNCED TERRIBLE THIRD-QUARTER RESULTS, HE LAY FOR HOURS IN THE DARK ON THE FLOOR OF A CONFERENCE ROOM.

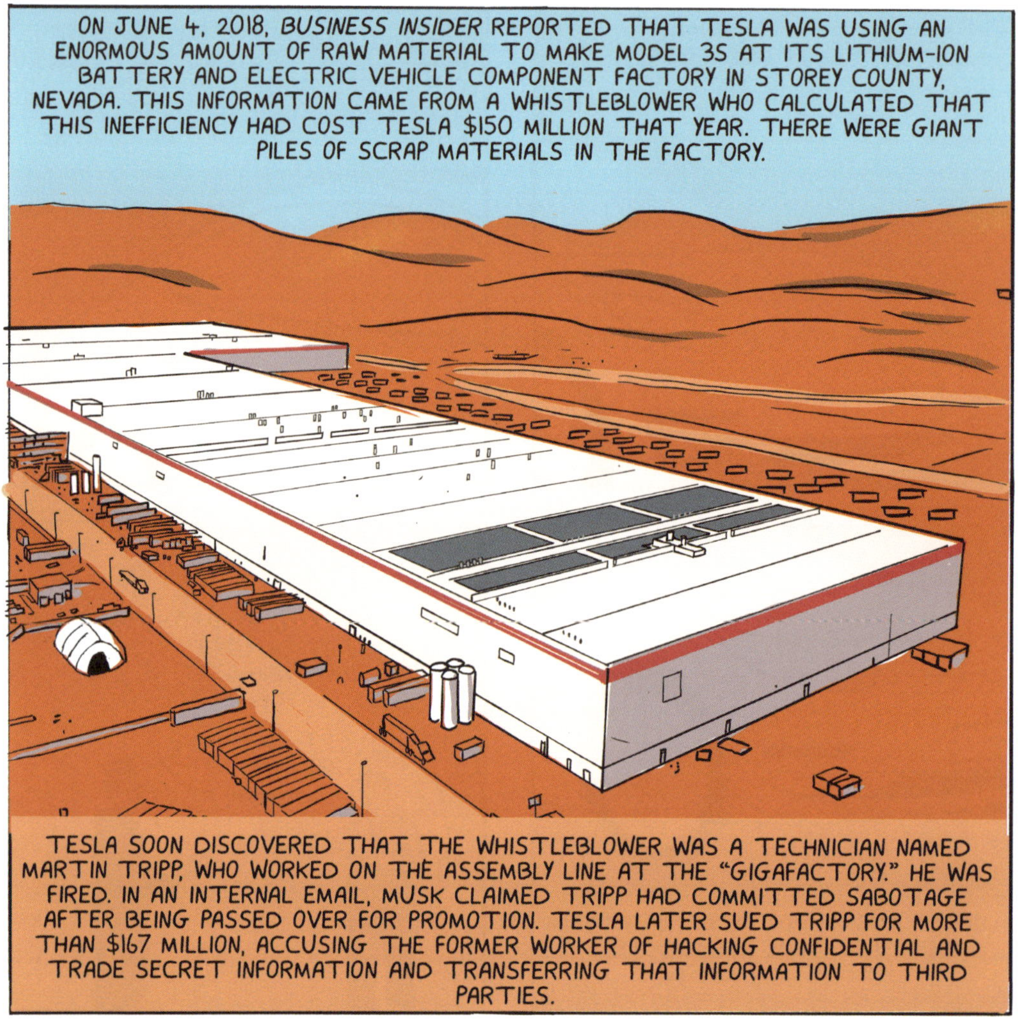
ON JUNE 4, 2018, *BUSINESS INSIDER* REPORTED THAT TESLA WAS USING AN ENORMOUS AMOUNT OF RAW MATERIAL TO MAKE MODEL 3S AT ITS LITHIUM-ION BATTERY AND ELECTRIC VEHICLE COMPONENT FACTORY IN STOREY COUNTY, NEVADA. THIS INFORMATION CAME FROM A WHISTLEBLOWER WHO CALCULATED THAT THIS INEFFICIENCY HAD COST TESLA $150 MILLION THAT YEAR. THERE WERE GIANT PILES OF SCRAP MATERIALS IN THE FACTORY.
TESLA SOON DISCOVERED THAT THE WHISTLEBLOWER WAS A TECHNICIAN NAMED MARTIN TRIPP, WHO WORKED ON THE ASSEMBLY LINE AT THE "GIGAFACTORY." HE WAS FIRED. IN AN INTERNAL EMAIL, MUSK CLAIMED TRIPP HAD COMMITTED SABOTAGE AFTER BEING PASSED OVER FOR PROMOTION. TESLA LATER SUED TRIPP FOR MORE THAN $167 MILLION, ACCUSING THE FORMER WORKER OF HACKING CONFIDENTIAL AND TRADE SECRET INFORMATION AND TRANSFERRING THAT INFORMATION TO THIRD PARTIES.

THE LAWSUIT ALSO CLAIMED THAT TRIPP INSTALLED SOFTWARE ON THE COMPUTERS OF THREE COLLEAGUES SO THAT DATA CONTINUED TO BE EXPORTED AFTER HE LEFT THE COMPANY. THIS ACT WOULD HAVE FRAMED HIS FORMER COWORKERS.
MARTIN TRIPP.

TRIPP COUNTERED THAT HE'D NEVER HACKED THE INFORMATION. HE'D JUST SEARCHED THE DATABASE AND ONLY LEAKED IT BECAUSE HE WAS CONCERNED ABOUT PUBLIC SAFETY.
I DON'T KNOW HOW TO CODE. I DON'T HAVE THE PATIENCE.

THE SAME DAY TRIPP LEARNED HE WAS BEING SUED BY TESLA, THE COMPANY CLAIMED AN ANONYMOUS FRIEND OF TRIPP HAD CALLED THEM TO SAY THEIR FORMER EMPLOYEE WAS PLANNING A MASS SHOOTING AT THE FACTORY.
WHAT?
THE SECURITY MANAGER AT THE GIGAFACTORY, SEAN GOUTHRO (WHO LATER BECAME A TESLA WHISTLEBLOWER HIMSELF) CLAIMED TESLA BEHAVED UNETHICALLY AGAINST TRIPP.
ACCORDING TO GOUTHRO, INVESTIGATORS HIRED BY TESLA, ALLEGEDLY HACKED TRIPP'S PHONE AND FOLLOWED HIM.
ON THE EVENING OF THE ANONYMOUS TIP, TESLA'S INVESTIGATORS FOUND TRIPP BEFORE THE SHERIFF'S DEPARTMENT DID, TRACKING HIM TO THE NUGGET CASINO IN RENO, NEVADA.
NUGGET
DEPUTIES MET TRIPP OUTSIDE THE CASINO WHERE THEY DETERMINED THERE WAS NO CREDIBLE THREAT.
I'M NOT ARMED.
GOUTHRO BELIEVES THAT TESLA SPREAD MISINFORMATION ABOUT TRIPP TO RUIN HIS LIFE BEYOND THE MASS SHOOTING ALLEGATION.

IN JULY 2018 TRIPP COUNTERSUED TESLA, MAINTAINING THAT THE COMPANY HAD PUBLISHED FALSE AND DEFAMATORY STATEMENTS OUT OF MALICE, WITH THE AIM OF RETALIATION.
THIS DEFAMATION CLAIM WAS DISMISSED IN SEPTEMBER 2020 BY NEVADA JUDGE MIRANDA DU.
TRIPP CANNOT SHOW ACTUAL MALICE. INDEED, THE COURT FINDS HE CANNOT EVEN MEET THE LOWER BAR OF FALSITY.
TESLA WON THEIR CASE AGAINST TRIPP IN DECEMBER THAT YEAR, BUT DIDN'T GET THEIR $167 MILLION IN DAMAGES.
TRIPP WAS ORDERED TO PAY $400,000, PLUS A PAYMENT OF $25,000 FOR CONTINUING TO SHARE INFORMATION ABOUT TESLA AFTER BEING ORDERED TO STOP BY A JUDGE.
THIS WASN'T THE ONLY LEGAL ISSUE MUSK AND TESLA HAD TO DEAL WITH DURING THIS PERIOD.
ARE YOU MUSK?
YES.
IN 2018, MUSK WAS SUED BY THE SECURITIES AND EXCHANGE COMMISSION (SEC) FOR WRITING ON THE SOCIAL MEDIA SITE TWITTER THAT FUNDING HAD BEEN SECURED TO POTENTIALLY TAKE TESLA PRIVATE AT $420 PER SHARE.
WE BELIEVE YOU'VE COMMITTED SECURITIES FRAUD.

ACCORDING TO THE SEC'S COMPLAINT, MUSK'S MISLEADING TWEETS CAUSED TESLA'S STOCK PRICE TO JUMP BY OVER SIX PERCENT, WHICH LED TO SIGNIFICANT MARKET DISRUPTION.
TWO DAYS LATER, MUSK HAD SETTLED WITH THE SEC WITHOUT ADMITTING OR DENYING THE ALLEGATIONS.
I'M SAYING NOTHING.
MUSK AND TESLA WERE FINED $20 MILLION EACH, AND MUSK WAS OBLIGED TO STEP DOWN FROM HIS POSITION AS TESLA CHAIRMAN AND BE INELIGIBLE FOR RE-ELECTION FOR THREE YEARS. HE REMAINED AS CEO.
GIVE.
$
THE $40 MILLION IN PENALTIES WERE DISTRIBUTED TO INVESTORS.
OTHER SEC REQUIREMENTS INCLUDED TWO NEW INDEPENDENT DIRECTORS ADDED TO TESLA'S BOARD AND EXTRA CONTROLS AND PROCEDURES TO OVERSEE MUSK'S COMMUNICATIONS.
IN JULY 2018, MUSK GOT HIMSELF INTO FURTHER LEGAL TROUBLE, AND AGAIN IT WAS BECAUSE OF A TWEET.

ON JUNE 23, 2018, TWELVE MEMBERS OF A JUNIOR ASSOCIATION SOCCER TEAM, AGED ELEVEN TO SIXTEEN, AND THEIR 25-YEAR-OLD ASSISTANT COACH, ENTERED THE THAM LUANG NANG NON CAVE IN CHIANG RAI PROVINCE IN NORTHERN THAILAND AFTER A PRACTICE SESSION.

SOON AFTER THEY ENTERED THE CAVE, TORRENTIAL RAINS CAUSED FLOODING, TRAPPING THEM ALL.

AN ENORMOUS INTERNATIONAL RESCUE EFFORT THEN BEGAN. HUNDREDS OF VOLUNTEERS, MILITARY SPECIALISTS, AND CORPORATE EXPERTS FROM AROUND THE WORLD OFFERED ASSISTANCE.

ELON MUSK SENT SPACEX AND BORING COMPANY ENGINEERS TO THAILAND. THE IDEA OF USING A CHILD-SIZED SUBMARINE THAT COULD SHUTTLE THE TRAPPED BOYS TO SAFETY CREATED OUT OF THE LIQUID OXYGEN TRANSFER TUBE FROM A FALCON ROCKET WAS DISCUSSED.
CAVE ENTRANCE.
AREA WHERE THE BOYS WERE TRAPPED.

ON JULY 8, A VIDEO OF THE SUBMARINE BEING TESTED WAS RELEASED.
THE NEXT DAY MUSK ARRIVED AT THE RESCUE SITE. HE STATED THAT THE MINI-SUB WAS READY IF NEEDED, AND IF NOT, MUSK HOPED IT WOULD BE USEFUL IN A "FUTURE SITUATION."
BUT IT WASN'T NEEDED. ALL TWELVE BOYS AND THEIR COACH WERE RESCUED ON JULY 10 WHEN DIVERS CARRIED THE BOYS—WHO WERE EQUIPPED WITH SCUBA MASKS—THROUGH THE WINDING, PARTIALLY SUBMERGED CAVE ON STRETCHERS.
IN THE AFTERMATH OF THE RESCUE AN UGLY WAR OF WORDS BROKE OUT BETWEEN MUSK AND VERNON UNSWORTH, A BRITISH MEMBER OF THE RESCUE EFFORT.
IN A CNN INTERVIEW, UNSWORTH DISPARAGED MUSK'S SUBMARINE PLAN, SAYING THAT...
IT HAD NO CHANCE OF WORKING.
THE RIGID SUBMARINE WOULDN'T HAVE MADE THE FIRST FIFTY METERS INTO THE CAVE.

IT WAS JUST A PR STUNT. HE CAN STICK HIS SUBMARINE WHERE IT HURTS.
THESE COMMENTS ENRAGED MUSK. HE TOOK TO TWITTER TO SAY HE DIDN'T RECALL SEEING UNSWORTH AT THE RESCUE SITE. HE THEN CALLED UNSWORTH A "PEDO GUY."
A WHAT?
IT LATER CAME TO LIGHT THAT MUSK HAD HIRED A PRIVATE INVESTI-GATOR TO LOOK INTO UNSWORTH'S BACKGROUND. THE INVESTIGATOR TURNED OUT TO BE A CON MAN WHO GAVE MUSK FALSE INFORMATION ABOUT THE CAVE DIVER.
?
TESLA'S STOCK PRICE FELL AFTER MUSK'S CONTROVERSIAL ACCUSATION.
MUSK ALSO EMAILED A *BUZZFEED* REPORTER WITH FALSE ACCUSATIONS THAT UNSWORTH WAS A CHILD RAPIST WITH A TWELVE-YEAR-OLD CHILD BRIDE. IT WAS AN OFF-THE-RECORD EMAIL THAT WAS PUBLISHED BY THE WEB-SITE ANYWAY.
IN A LATER TWEET, MUSK APOLO-GIZED TO UNSWORTH ABOUT HIS "PEDO GUY" REMARKS. BUT THIS DIDN'T STOP THE CAVE DIVER SUING THE CEO FOR $190 MILLION, ARGUING THAT HIS REPUTATION HAD BEEN DAMAGED. COURT DOCUMENTS WERE LATER TO REVEAL THAT MUSK THOUGHT HIMSELF "A FUCKING IDIOT" IN THIS AFFAIR.

THE FOUR-DAY LIBEL TRIAL TOOK PLACE IN A LOS ANGELES COURTROOM IN DECEMBER 2019. THE DEFENSE ARGUED...
THE TWEET WAS AN INSULT, NOT A STATEMENT OF FACT, AND THEREFORE SHOULD BE CONSIDERED PROTECTED SPEECH.
THEY ALSO CLAIMED...
UNSWORTH'S REPUTATION HAS NOT BEEN UNDULY DAMAGED, BECAUSE HIS EFFORTS IN THE RESCUE OPERATION WERE REWARDED WITH A MEMBER OF THE ORDER OF THE BRITISH EMPIRE, AND A MEDAL FROM THE THAI KING, AMONG OTHER HONORS.
IN UNSWORTH'S TESTIMONY, HE SAID...
BEING BRANDED A PEDOPHILE MADE ME FEEL HUMILIATED, ASHAMED, DIRTY.
I WAS EFFECTIVELY GIVEN A LIFE SENTENCE WITHOUT PAROLE. IT HURTS TO TALK ABOUT IT.
THE JURY DELIBERATED FOR LESS THAN AN HOUR BEFORE FINDING IN FAVOR OF MUSK, RULING HE WAS NOT LIABLE.
MUSK HAD WON AGAIN.

FEBRUARY 6, 2018, SAW THE FIRST FLIGHT OF SPACEX'S FALCON HEAVY ROCKET, A PARTIALLY REUSABLE SUPER HEAVY-LIFT LAUNCH VEHICLE, DESIGNED TO CARRY CARGO INTO EARTH ORBIT AND BEYOND.
THE ROCKET WAS COMPOSED OF THREE REUSABLE FALCON 9 FIRST-STAGE BOOSTERS STRAPPED TOGETHER SIDE BY SIDE, CREATING THE MOST POWERFUL OPERATIONAL ROCKET AT THAT TIME.
THE TWO SIDE BOOSTERS RETURNED SUCCESSFULLY TO EARTH, MAKING IMPRESSIVE PARALLEL TOUCHDOWNS AT LANDING ZONES ONE AND TWO AT CAPE CANAVERAL AIR FORCE STATION (RENAMED CAPE CANAVERAL SPACE FORCE STATION).

THE CENTRAL BOOSTER WAS DESTROYED WHEN WHEN TWO OF ITS ENGINES FAILED TO IGNITE DURING DESCENT...

...AND AS A RESULT OF THIS, IT SLAMMED INTO THE OCEAN AT A SPEED OF OVER 300 MILES AN HOUR, DAMAGING THE NEARBY DRONE SHIP IT WAS SUPPOSED TO LAND ON.

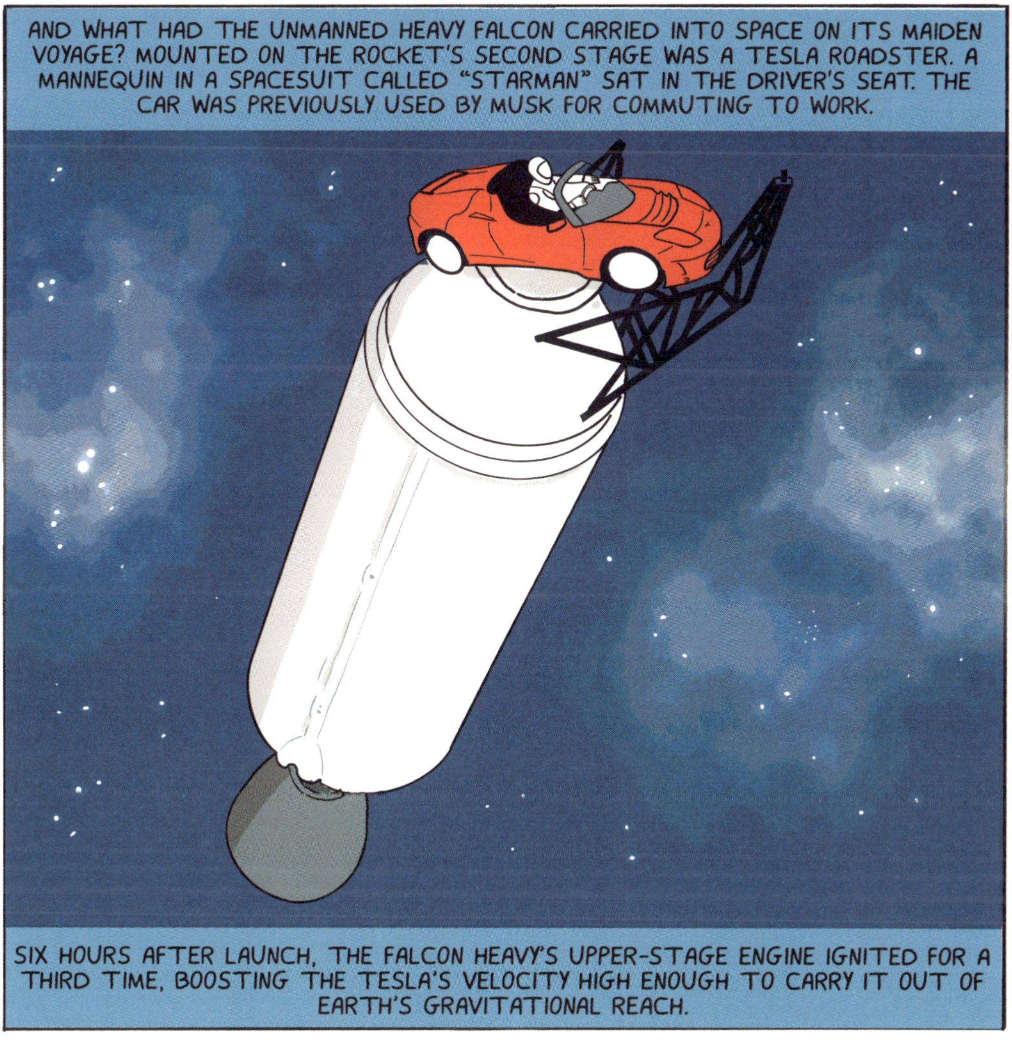
AND WHAT HAD THE UNMANNED HEAVY FALCON CARRIED INTO SPACE ON ITS MAIDEN VOYAGE? MOUNTED ON THE ROCKET'S SECOND STAGE WAS A TESLA ROADSTER. A MANNEQUIN IN A SPACESUIT CALLED "STARMAN" SAT IN THE DRIVER'S SEAT. THE CAR WAS PREVIOUSLY USED BY MUSK FOR COMMUTING TO WORK.
SIX HOURS AFTER LAUNCH, THE FALCON HEAVY'S UPPER-STAGE ENGINE IGNITED FOR A THIRD TIME, BOOSTING THE TESLA'S VELOCITY HIGH ENOUGH TO CARRY IT OUT OF EARTH'S GRAVITATIONAL REACH.

AT THE 2018 SOUTH BY SOUTHWEST FESTIVAL IN AUSTIN, TEXAS, MUSK EXPLAINED HIS REASONS FOR THE STUNT.
SXSW 2018
THE GOAL OF THIS WAS TO INSPIRE YOU AND MAKE YOU BELIEVE AGAIN, JUST AS PEOPLE BELIEVED IN THE APOLLO ERA, THAT ANYTHING IS POSSIBLE.
BEFORE LAUNCH, THE CAR'S SOUND SYSTEM WAS SET TO CONTINUOUSLY PLAY THE DAVID BOWIE SONG "SPACE ODDITY."
IN THE GLOVEBOX THERE WAS A COPY OF DOUGLAS ADAMS' NOVEL *THE HITCHHIKER'S GUIDE TO THE GALAXY*. THE CAR ALSO CARRIED A COPY OF ISAAC ASIMOV'S *FOUNDATION TRILOGY* ON A 5D OPTICAL DISC.
THE ROADSTER'S ORBIT AROUND THE SUN TOOK IT OUT BEYOND MARS, THEN BACK TO SWING PAST THE EARTH.
A COSMIC LOOP THAT WILL REPEAT FOR THOUSANDS OF YEARS.

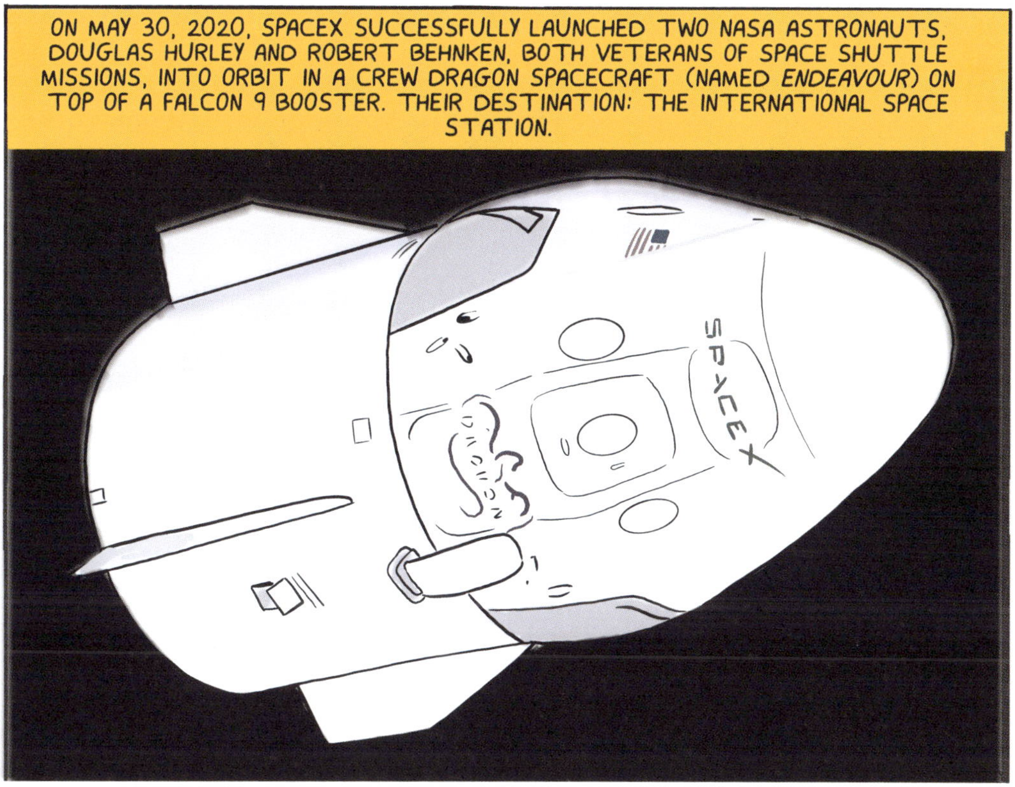
ON MAY 30, 2020, SPACEX SUCCESSFULLY LAUNCHED TWO NASA ASTRONAUTS, DOUGLAS HURLEY AND ROBERT BEHNKEN, BOTH VETERANS OF SPACE SHUTTLE MISSIONS, INTO ORBIT IN A CREW DRAGON SPACECRAFT (NAMED *ENDEAVOUR*) ON TOP OF A FALCON 9 BOOSTER. THEIR DESTINATION: THE INTERNATIONAL SPACE STATION.
SPACEX

THE LAUNCH WAS THE FIRST CREWED ORBITAL SPACEFLIGHT FROM THE UNITED STATES SINCE THE FINAL SPACE SHUTTLE MISSION IN 2011 AND THE FIRST TIME A COMMERCIAL OPERATOR HAD CARRIED ASTRONAUTS INTO SPACE.

THE RICHEST MAN IN THE WORLD

ELON MUSK BECAME THE RICHEST PERSON IN THE WORLD IN JANUARY 2021, WITH A NET WORTH OF OVER $185 BILLION, SURPASSING AMAZON FOUNDER JEFF BEZOS. BEZOS BRIEFLY RECLAIMED THE TITLE THE FOLLOWING MONTH, BUT THEN MUSK BECAME THE FIRST PERSON TO BE WORTH OVER $300 BILLION WHEN TESLA STOCK SURGED.
DID ELON MUSK HAVE TIME FOR A PERSONAL LIFE WHILE BUILDING THIS FORTUNE? YES.
MUSK WAS LINKED WITH ACTRESS AMBER HEARD FOR SEVERAL MONTHS IN 2017.

THEN, IN 2018, HE BEGAN DATING CANADIAN MUSICIAN, SINGER, SONGWRITER, AND RECORD PRODUCER GRIMES.
GRIMES GAVE BIRTH TO THEIR SON IN MAY 2020. THE BOY WAS EVENTUALLY NAMED X AE A-XII MUSK.
HOW DO YOU PRONOUNCE THAT, MR. MUSK?
X IS JUST PRONOUNCED X. AE IS PRONOUNCED ASH. A-XII IS THE ROMAN NUMERAL VERSION OF A-12, NAMED AFTER MY FAVORITE AIRCRAFT, THE LOCKHEED A-12.
GRIMES AND MUSK HAD A SECOND CHILD IN DECEMBER 2021, A DAUGHTER NAMED EXA DARK SIDERAEL MUSK, BORN VIA SURROGACY.
WE CALL HER Y.
THE COUPLE'S RELATIONSHIP HAD BEGUN A PROCESS OF ENDING BY THEN. BOTH CLAIMED THEY REMAINED GOOD FRIENDS.
THE FOLLOWING YEAR IT CAME TO LIGHT THAT MUSK HAD TWO MORE CHILDREN: TWINS BY NEURALINK EXECUTIVE SHIVON ZILIS, CONCEIVED VIA IN VITRO FERTILIZATION.

ZILIS CLAIMED THAT...
I WASN'T INVOLVED ROMANTICALLY WITH MUSK.
NOT ALL OF MUSK'S CHILDREN HAVE A GOOD RELATIONSHIP WITH HIM.
WORLD'S WORST DAD
IN APRIL 2022, XAVIER ALEXANDER MUSK PETITIONED FOR BOTH A NAME CHANGE AND A NEW BIRTH CERTIFICATE AT THE LOS ANGELES COUNTY SUPERIOR COURT IN SANTA MONICA, CALIFORNIA. THE EIGHTEEN-YEAR-OLD ASKED TO BE RECOGNIZED AS FEMALE AND KNOWN BY THE NAME VIVIAN JENNA WILSON.
COURT DOCUMENTS LIST THE REASONS FOR THE NAME CHANGE AS: GENDER IDENTITY AND THE FACT THAT...
I NO LONGER LIVE WITH OR WISH TO BE RELATED TO MY BIOLOGICAL FATHER IN ANY WAY, SHAPE, OR FORM.
IN A *FINANCIAL TIMES* INTERVIEW IN OCTOBER 2022, MUSK BLAMED THE RIFT WITH HIS DAUGHTER ON THE TAKEOVER OF ELITE SCHOOLS AND UNIVERSITIES BY NEO-MARXISTS.
THEY TEACH IF YOU'RE RICH, YOU'RE EVIL.

IN HIS POLITICS, MUSK SEEMS TO HAVE CLAIMED TO BE A CENTRIST, NEITHER ON THE LEFT NOR RIGHT.
I BELIEVE IN FREE SPEECH AND HEALTHY DEBATE.
BUT MUSK'S PUBLIC STATEMENTS AND ACTIONS IN RECENT YEARS TELL A DIFFERENT STORY. HE APPEARS DEEPLY COMMITTED TO THE RIGHT'S CULTURE WAR AGAINST PROGRESSIVISM.
L
R
IT WAS NOT ALWAYS THIS WAY. THERE WAS A TIME WHEN HE APPEARED TO BE GENUINELY MORE OF A CENTRIST, OR WAS IT JUST HIS WAY OF COURTING DEMOCRATS IN ATTEMPT TO GAIN ACCESS TO LUCRATIVE GOVERNMENT CONTRACTS?
SPACEX
IN 2011 HE DONATED $35,800 TO THE OBAMA VICTORY FUND FOR THE PRESIDENT'S REELECTION BID AND ALSO DONATED $30,800 TO THE DEMOCRATIC NATIONAL COMMITTEE.
IN 2015 HE DONATED $5,000 TO HELP FUND HILLARY CLINTON'S CAMPAIGN FOR PRESIDENT. IN 2016 HE VOCALLY SUPPORTED CLINTON AND DENOUNCED HER OPPONENT DONALD TRUMP, SAYING...
TRUMP DOESN'T HAVE THE SORT OF CHARACTER THAT REFLECTS WELL ON THE UNITED STATES.

AFTER TRUMP WAS ELECTED, MUSK SERVED FOR AROUND FIVE MONTHS ON TWO PRESIDENTIAL ADVISORY COUNCILS—THE STRATEGIC AND POLICY FORUM AND THE MANUFACTURING JOBS INITIATIVE—BUT HE RESIGNED FROM BOTH IN PROTEST WHEN THE ADMINISTRATION PULLED OUT OF THE PARIS CLIMATE ACCORD. MUSK WROTE ON TWITTER THAT HE BELIEVED CLIMATE CHANGE TO BE REAL AND THAT LEAVING THE PARIS AGREEMENT WAS NOT GOOD FOR AMERICA OR THE WORLD.
BY 2022 MUSK'S BIPARTISAN APPROACH TO POLITICS WAS OVER. HE WROTE ON TWITTER THAT HE'D...
...VOTED DEMOCRAT IN THE PAST, BECAUSE THEY WERE MOSTLY THE KINDNESS PARTY, BUT NOW THAT THEY'VE BECOME THE PARTY OF DIVISION AND HATE, I'LL VOTE REPUBLICAN.
THIS STATEMENT CAME AROUND THE SAME TIME HIS TRANS CHILD DISOWNED HIM. DID THIS VERY PERSONAL FAMILY DISPUTE RADICALIZE MUSK, TRIGGERING HIS ABRUPT PUBLIC SPLIT FROM LEFT-LEANING POLITICS?
ONLY MUSK CAN SAY, BUT FROM THIS POINT ONWARDS HE BECAME INCREASINGLY RIGHT-WING IN HIS PRONOUNCEMENTS...
...ESPECIALLY ON SOCIAL ISSUES.
THE WOKE MIND VIRUS IS GOING TO DESTROY CIVILIZATION.

MUSK'S VIEWS ON LGBTQ ISSUES ARE CONTRADICTORY. HE'S EXPRESSED SUPPORT FOR THE TRANS COMMUNITY, BUT AT THE SAME TIME MOCKED THE PRACTICE OF DISPLAYING PRONOUNS ON SOCIAL MEDIA AND IN BIOS.
PRONOUNS SUCK.
AND HE OPPOSED GENDER-DYSPHORIC CHILDREN UNDERGOING GENDER-AFFIRMING MEDICAL PROCEDURES (WHICH ARE CONSIDERED BEST PRACTICE BY THE AMERICAN MEDICAL ASSOCIATION, THE CHILDREN'S HOSPITAL ASSOCIATION, AND THE AMERICAN ACADEMY OF PEDIATRICS).
A PARENT OR DOCTOR WHO STERILIZES A CHILD SHOULD GO TO PRISON FOR LIFE.
DURING THE COVID-19 PANDEMIC, MUSK JOINED MANY ON THE POLITICAL RIGHT IN DISPUTING THE SERIOUSNESS OF THE VIRUS AND THE EFFECTIVENESS OF THE VARIOUS VACCINES.
IN 2020, AS GLOBALLY COVID-19 CASES HIT 100,000 AND DEATHS BEGAN TO EXCEED 3,000, HE WROTE ON TWITTER...
THE CORONAVIRUS PANIC IS DUMB.
MUSK PREDICTED THE US WOULD HAVE "CLOSE TO ZERO NEW CASES" BY THE END OF APRIL. BUT WHEN THAT DATE WAS REACHED DAILY CASE COUNTS HAD REACHED 20,000.

MUSK TOLD KARA SWISHER OF *THE NEW YORK TIMES* THAT HE WOULDN'T TAKE A COVID-19 VACCINE, ARGUING HE AND HIS KIDS ARE NOT AT RISK AND THAT THE VIRUS HAS A LOW MORTALITY RATE.
THE WORLD HEALTH ORGANIZATION ESTIMATED THAT THE TOTAL NUMBER OF GLOBAL DEATHS ATTRIBUTED TO COVID-19 IN 2020 WAS AT LEAST THREE MILLION. THAT'S FAR FROM A LOW MORTALITY RATE.
ON TWITTER HE WROTE...
KIDS ARE ESSENTIALLY IMMUNE.
MUSK EVENTUALLY DID TAKE THE VACCINE. HE WROTE ON TWITTER IN EARLY 2023...
I HAD MAJOR SIDE EFFECTS FROM MY SECOND BOOSTER SHOT. FELT LIKE I WAS DYING FOR SEVERAL DAYS.
CHILDREN CAN GET AND DO TRANSMIT COVID-19. SERIOUS SIDE EFFECTS FROM THE VACCINE DO HAPPEN, BUT THEY ARE RARE. FOR SOMEONE WHO CLAIMS TO HAVE A SCIENCE-BASED APPROACH TO LIFE, MUSK SEEMED KEEN TO IGNORE THE EVIDENCE. HE DOWNPLAYED THE SERIOUSNESS OF THE PANDEMIC AS MUCH AS HE COULD AND RESISTED SHUTTING THE TESLA FACTORY IN CALIFORNIA DURING THE LOCKDOWN.
TESLA

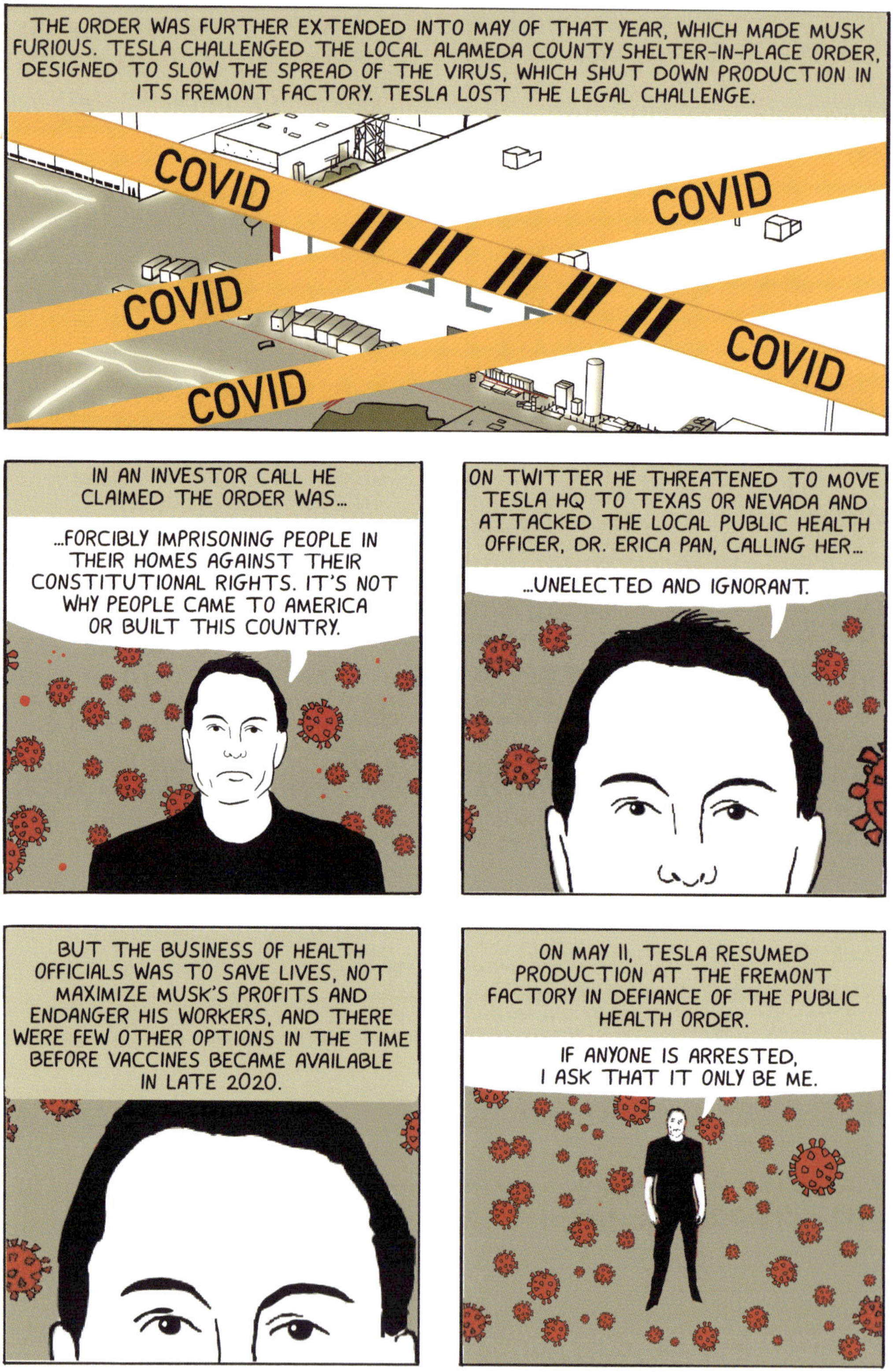
THE ORDER WAS FURTHER EXTENDED INTO MAY OF THAT YEAR, WHICH MADE MUSK FURIOUS. TESLA CHALLENGED THE LOCAL ALAMEDA COUNTY SHELTER-IN-PLACE ORDER, DESIGNED TO SLOW THE SPREAD OF THE VIRUS, WHICH SHUT DOWN PRODUCTION IN ITS FREMONT FACTORY. TESLA LOST THE LEGAL CHALLENGE.
COVID
COVID
COVID
COVID
COVID
IN AN INVESTOR CALL HE CLAIMED THE ORDER WAS...
...FORCIBLY IMPRISONING PEOPLE IN THEIR HOMES AGAINST THEIR CONSTITUTIONAL RIGHTS. IT'S NOT WHY PEOPLE CAME TO AMERICA OR BUILT THIS COUNTRY.
ON TWITTER HE THREATENED TO MOVE TESLA HQ TO TEXAS OR NEVADA AND ATTACKED THE LOCAL PUBLIC HEALTH OFFICER, DR. ERICA PAN, CALLING HER...
...UNELECTED AND IGNORANT.
BUT THE BUSINESS OF HEALTH OFFICIALS WAS TO SAVE LIVES, NOT MAXIMIZE MUSK'S PROFITS AND ENDANGER HIS WORKERS, AND THERE WERE FEW OTHER OPTIONS IN THE TIME BEFORE VACCINES BECAME AVAILABLE IN LATE 2020.
ON MAY 11, TESLA RESUMED PRODUCTION AT THE FREMONT FACTORY IN DEFIANCE OF THE PUBLIC HEALTH ORDER.
IF ANYONE IS ARRESTED, I ASK THAT IT ONLY BE ME.

NO ONE WAS ARRESTED. THE NEXT DAY ALAMEDA COUNTY ANNOUNCED THAT AFTER REVIEWING TESLA'S SAFETY PLAN, THEY AGREED THAT TESLA COULD REOPEN "AS SOON AS NEXT WEEK."
COUNTY OF ALAMEDA
CALIFORNIA
WE WILL BE WORKING WITH THE FREMONT POLICE DEPARTMENT TO VERIFY TESLA IS ADHERING TO PHYSICAL DISTANCING AND THAT AGREED-UPON HEALTH AND SAFETY MEASURES ARE IN PLACE FOR THEIR WORKERS AS THEY PREPARE FOR FULL PRODUCTION.
COUNTY OF ALAMEDA
CALIFORNIA
IN 2022, MUSK CALLED FOR THE PROSECUTION OF DR. ANTHONY FAUCI, THE US'S LEADING IMMUNOLOGIST AND WHITE HOUSE ADVISOR FOR THE COVID-19 PANDEMIC, IN A TWITTER POST THAT ALSO MANAGED TO DISRESPECT TRANSGENDER AND NON-BINARY PEOPLE.
MY PRONOUNS ARE PROSECUTE/FAUCI.
?
FURTHER TWEETS SUGGESTED THAT MUSK HAD BOUGHT INTO THE RIGHT-WING CONSPIRACY THEORY THAT THE VIRUS HAD LEAKED FROM A LAB IN WUHAN, THE CHINESE CITY WHERE IT WAS FIRST DETECTED...
...AND THAT HE BELIEVED FAUCI HAD LIED TO CONGRESS ABOUT US FUNDING OF RESEARCH AT THE WUHAN LAB, WHICH HAD MADE THE VIRUS MORE INFECTIOUS.
RESEARCH THAT KILLED MILLIONS OF PEOPLE.

DID THE US FUND VIRUS RESEARCH IN CHINA? THE US NATIONAL INSTITUTE OF ALLERGY AND INFECTIOUS DISEASES (NIAID), OF WHICH DR. FAUCI WAS THE DIRECTOR, AWARDED A GRANT TO THE US-BASED ECOHEALTHALLIANCE TO LOOK INTO THE DANGER OF CORONAVIRUSES FROM BATS.
DR. RALPH BARIC FROM THE UNIVERSITY OF NORTH CAROLINA WAS ONE OF THE US SCIENTISTS WHO COLLABORATED ON THE 2015 RESEARCH ON BAT VIRUSES WITH THE WUHAN INSTITUTE OF VIROLOGY.
HE GAVE A DETAILED STATEMENT TO *THE WASHINGTON POST*, SAYING...
THE WORK WE DID WAS REVIEWED BY BOTH THE NATIONAL INSTITUTES OF HEALTH (NIH) AND THE UNIVERSITY'S OWN BIOSAFETY COMMITTEE, AND DEEMED NOT TO BE GAIN-OF-FUNCTION.
MEANING THAT THE WORK DID NOT INCREASE THE TRANSMISSIBILITY OR VIRULENCE OF THE MICROORGANISMS UNDER STUDY.
BARIC ALSO STATED THAT NONE OF THE VIRUSES THAT WERE THE SUBJECT OF THE STUDY WERE RELATED TO SARS-COV-2, THE CAUSE OF THE 2020 PANDEMIC.

WHILE MUSK RAGED AGAINST LOCKDOWN WORKPLACE PROTECTIONS IN THE US, WHEN TESLA'S ENORMOUS GIGAFACTORY IN SHANGHAI WAS SHUTTERED BY AUTHORITIES IN CHINA, HE DIDN'T CONDEMN THIS ACTION.
THE FACTORY LATER REOPENED UNDER RULES THAT INCLUDED HAVING WORKERS TEMPORARILY LIVE AT THE PLANT. THEY WERE NOT ALLOWED TO RETURN TO THEIR HOMES.
MUSK SAID NOTHING PUBLICLY ABOUT THIS. COULD THE REASON FOR HIS SILENCE BE THAT HE DIDN'T WANT TO UPSET THE CHINESE GOVERNMENT WHEN THAT COUNTRY WAS TESLA'S SECOND BIGGEST MARKET?
ALTHOUGH ALWAYS KEEN TO PORTRAY HIMSELF AS A FREE SPEECH ADVOCATE, MUSK WAS HAPPY TO WRITE AN ARTICLE FOR *CHINA CYBERSPACE*—THE OFFICIAL PUBLICATION OF THE CYBERSPACE ADMINISTRATION OF CHINA.
2
Q
A
THE BODY THAT ENFORCES INTERNET CENSORSHIP IN CHINA.
IN 2022, MUSK SUGGESTED GIVING CHINA SOME CONTROL OVER TAIWAN IN ORDER TO RESOLVE THE DISPUTE BETWEEN THE TWO COUNTRIES.
CHINA
TAIWAN

THE ISLAND OF TAIWAN, INDEPENDENT SINCE 1950, IS REGARDED AS A BREAKAWAY PROVINCE BY CHINA. CHINA'S PRESIDENT XI JINPING HAS SAID "REUNIFICATION" WITH TAIWAN "MUST BE FULFILLED." HE HAS NOT RULED OUT MILITARY ACTION.
TAIWAN'S AMBASSADOR TO THE US, HSIAO BI-KHIM, RESPONDED TO MUSK'S COMMENTS...
FREEDOM AND DEMOCRACY ARE NOT FOR SALE.
ANY LASTING PROPOSAL FOR OUR FUTURE MUST BE DETERMINED PEACEFULLY, FREE FROM COERCION, AND RESPECTFUL OF THE DEMOCRATIC WISHES OF THE PEOPLE OF TAIWAN.
MUSK'S COMMENTS ON TAIWAN SEEM TO BE PART OF A PATTERN OF DEFERENCE TO AUTHORITARIAN REGIMES HE INDULGES IN WHEN IT AIDS HIS BUSINESS INTERESTS.
WE WOULD SEE THIS AGAIN AFTER MUSK'S PURCHASE OF THE SOCIAL MEDIA COMPANY TWITTER IN 2022.

FOR MUSK, TWITTER HAD BECOME AN IMPORTANT PART OF HIS BRAND. OVER THIRTEEN YEARS, HE'D USED THE PLATFORM TO BUILD UP A FOLLOWING OF MORE THAN EIGHTY MILLION PEOPLE.
ON TWITTER, HE WROTE ABOUT HIS BUSINESS VENTURES, BERATED HIS CRITICS, AND SHARED MEMES.
I LOVE TWITTER.
HE REPEATEDLY STATED THAT HIS GOAL IN BUYING TWITTER WAS TO MAKE IT A PLATFORM FOR FREE SPEECH. TWITTER SHOULD BE...
...A COMMON DIGITAL TOWN SQUARE, WHERE A WIDE RANGE OF BELIEFS CAN BE DEBATED IN A HEALTHY MANNER.
BUT MUSK'S STATEMENTS SUGGESTED TO MANY THAT WHAT HE REALLY WANTED WAS A PLATFORM MORE FAVORABLE TO THOSE ON THE EXTREMES OF THE POLITICAL RIGHT.
DOES A WIDE RANGE OF BELIEFS INCLUDE OURS?
MANY OF WHOM WERE AT THAT TIME SUSPENDED FROM TWITTER BECAUSE THEY'D BEEN FOUND GUILTY OF SPREADING MISINFORMATION, OR HAD INDULGED IN PERSONAL HARASSMENT OR HATE SPEECH.
!
ACCOUNT SUSPENDED
THOSE SUSPENDED INCLUDED *THE BABYLON BEE*, A CONSERVATIVE CHRISTIAN NEWS SATIRE WEBSITE THAT WAS LOCKED OUT OF ITS ACCOUNT FOR TWEETING...
...THE *BABYLON BEE'S* MAN OF THE YEAR IS RACHEL LEVINE.

A REFERENCE TO THE THEN US ASSISTANT SECRETARY FOR HEALTH, A TRANSGENDER WOMAN.
JORDAN PETERSON, A CONSERVATIVE PSYCHOLOGIST AND SELF-HELP AUTHOR, WAS SUSPENDED FOR REFERRING TO ACTOR ELLIOT PAGE BY HIS FORMER FEMALE NAME WHICH VIOLATED TWITTER'S POLICIES ON HARASSMENT.
I DON'T CARE.
PRESIDENT DONALD TRUMP'S ACCOUNT WAS PERMANENTLY SUSPENDED DUE TO THE RISK OF FURTHER INCITEMENT OF VIOLENCE AFTER THE JANUARY 6 INSURRECTION WHEN THOUSANDS OF TRUMP SUPPORTERS STORMED THE US CONGRESS IN AN ATTEMPT TO STOP THE CERTIFICATION OF JOE BIDEN'S VICTORY IN THE 2020 PRESIDENTIAL ELECTION. FOUR CIVILIANS AND A POLICE OFFICER DIED.
SUCH BANNING ENRAGED PEOPLE ON THE POLITICAL RIGHT WHO'VE ARGUED FOR YEARS THAT SOCIAL MEDIA PLATFORMS DISPROPORTIONATELY STIFLE CONSERVATIVE SPEECH.
MAGA
I'VE BEEN CANCELLED.
ALTHOUGH RESEARCH FINDS CONSERVATIVE CONTENT IS SOME OF THE MORE WIDELY SHARED ON THE INTERNET.
SEE MY FACEBOOK PAGE, INSTAGRAM, YOUTUBE CHANNEL, AND APPEARANCES IN NATIONAL MEDIA FOR DETAILS.
MAGA

ON APRIL 5, 2022, IT WAS REVEALED THAT MUSK HAD BOUGHT MORE THAN 9 PERCENT OF TWITTER'S SHARES, MAKING HIM TWITTER'S BIGGEST OUTSIDE SHAREHOLDER.
TWITTER OFFERED MUSK A PLACE ON THE BOARD OF DIRECTORS.
WHERE I WOULDN'T BE ALLOWED TO BUY MORE THAN 14.9 PERCENT OF THE COMPANY.
IN THE END, MUSK DECLINED TO JOIN THE BOARD. ON APRIL 13 HE MADE AN OFFER TO BUY TWITTER FOR $54.20 A SHARE—A PRICE AROUND $44 BILLION—FAR ABOVE THE COMPANY'S STOCK PRICE.
I WANT IT ALL.
THE FUNDING FOR THE DEAL INCLUDED ABOUT $12.5 BILLION IN LOANS AGAINST HIS TESLA STOCK AND $21 BILLION IN EQUITY FINANCING (SALES OF SHARES).
WHAT COULD GO WRONG?
THE NEXT DAY TESLA'S STOCK MARKET VALUE SANK BY OVER $125 BILLION IN RESPONSE TO THE DEAL. MUSK LOST AROUND $30 BILLION OF HIS NET WORTH.
THUNK!

ON APRIL 25, TWITTER ANNOUNCED IT HAD DECIDED TO ACCEPT MUSK'S OFFER.
FOR SALE

BUT A COUPLE WEEKS LATER, MUSK ANNOUNCED THAT THE DEAL WAS "ON HOLD" WHILE HE WAITED FOR THE SOCIAL MEDIA COMPANY TO PROVIDE DATA ON THE PROPORTION OF ITS FAKE ACCOUNTS.
PROVE THAT LESS THAN 5% OF TWITTER ACCOUNTS ARE FAKE/SPAM.

ON JULY 12, TWITTER SUED MUSK FOR BREACHING A LEGALLY BINDING AGREEMENT TO PURCHASE TWITTER. MUSK COUNTERSUED, ACCUSING TWITTER OF FRAUD.
LAWSUIT
LAWSUIT

THE TWO SIDES WERE SCHEDULED TO MEET IN A DELAWARE COURTROOM, BUT THEN IN LATE OCTOBER, MUSK RE-SUBMITTED HIS ORIGINAL $44 BILLION OFFER, WITHOUT EXPLANATION.
SOLD

ON OCTOBER 28, MUSK TOOK OWNERSHIP OF TWITTER AND FIRED KEY EXECUTIVES, INCLUDING CEO PARAG AGRAWAL AND POLICY DIRECTOR VIJAYA GADDE.

HE POSTED A VIDEO OF HIMSELF ENTERING THE COMPANY'S SAN FRANCISCO LOBBY CARRYING A SINK.
LET THAT SINK IN.

MUSK IMMEDIATELY ELIMINATED ABOUT HALF OF TWITTER'S WORKFORCE, OR AROUND 3,700 JOBS. ENTIRE DEPARTMENTS WERE AXED, INCLUDING TEAMS MODERATING MISINFORMATION AND HUMAN RIGHTS.
MUSK TWEETED, "REGARDING TWITTER'S REDUCTION IN FORCE, UNFORTUNATELY THERE IS NO CHOICE WHEN THE COMPANY IS LOSING OVER $4M/DAY."
A NUMBER OF OF HIGH-PROFILE CELEBRITIES AND ACCOUNTS SUSPENDED BY TWITTER'S PREVIOUS ADMINISTRATION WERE REINSTATED TO THE SITE.
COME BACK.
THESE INCLUDED *THE BABYLON BEE*, JORDAN PETERSON, AND DONALD TRUMP. ALTHOUGH TRUMP DECLINED TO RETURN.
I'M ON THE RIGHT-WING SOCIAL MEDIA SITE TRUTH SOCIAL NOW.
ONE OF THE FIRST CHANGES MUSK MADE WAS TO TWITTER'S BLUE-CHECK MARK VERIFICATION SYSTEM.
THIS WAS A SYSTEM THAT PROVIDED A WAY OF DISTINGUISHING GENUINE NOTABLE ACCOUNT HOLDERS, SUCH AS CELEBRITIES AND ORGANIZATIONS, FROM IMPOSTORS OR PARODIES.

MUSK SCRAPPED THIS SYSTEM IN FAVOR OF A SUBSCRIPTION SERVICE, WHICH ALLOWED USERS TO ACCESS VERIFICATION FOR $8 A MONTH.
MUSK SAID THE SITE WOULD PERMANENTLY SUSPEND USERS WHO IMPERSONATED OTHERS, UNLESS THE ACCOUNT WAS MARKED AS A PARODY.
THIS POORLY THOUGHT-OUT IDEA WENT DISASTROUSLY WRONG IMMEDIATELY. TWITTER WAS FLOODED WITH FAKE ACCOUNTS IMPERSONATING PUBLIC FIGURES AND BRANDS—NONE MARKED AS PARODIES—WHICH THE NOW HOLLOWED OUT COMPANY STRUGGLED TO DEAL WITH.
WE DON'T HAVE THE STAFF.
SOME OF THE MOST OUTRAGEOUS IMPERSONATIONS FROM THE TWITTER BLUE ROLLOUT INCLUDED FORMER US PRESIDENT GEORGE W. BUSH.
I MISS KILLING IRAQIS.
FAKE TWEET.
US TEXAS SENATOR TED CRUZ.
I AM PRO-LIFE BECAUSE I FEAST ON NEGLECTED BABIES. NINE MONTHS AFTER PROM NIGHT I WANDER THE STREETS AND CHECK THE DUMPSTERS FOR DINNER, AND YOU WILL NOT BELIEVE HOW FRESH, AND HOW SWEET, THE MEAT IS.
FAKE TWEET.
THE COCA-COLA COMPANY.
IF THIS GETS 1000 RETWEETS WE WILL PUT COCAINE BACK IN COCA-COLA.
FAKE TWEET.
Coca-Cola

GIANT, ELI LILLY AND COMPANY.
WE ARE EXCITED TO ANNOUNCE INSULIN IS FREE NOW.
Lilly
FAKE TWEET.
OF COMPANIES SUSPENDED THEIR ADVERTISING ON THE PLATFORM, INCLUDING GENERAL MOTORS, GENERAL MILLS, AND VOLKSWAGEN.
WE ARE CLOSELY MONITORING THE SITUATION AND WILL DECIDE ABOUT NEXT STEPS DEPENDING ON ITS EVOLVEMENT.
TRUE STATEMENT.
VW
MUSK WAS OBLIGED TO PAUSE THE TWITTER "BLUE" ROLLOUT AND RELAUNCH IT A FEW WEEKS LATER.
AN ERROR OCCURED UPDATING TWITTER BLUE. TRY AGAIN?
OK
IN DECEMBER 2022, MUSK BEGAN RELEASING WHAT WAS DUBBED THE "TWITTER FILES."
A COLLECTION OF INTERNAL EMAILS AND CHATS SHOWING WHAT HAPPENED BEHIND THE SCENES REGARDING CONTENT-MODERATION DECISIONS AT TWITTER BEFORE I BOUGHT IT.
MUSK RELEASED THESE DOCUMENTS TO A HANDPICKED GROUP OF JOURNALISTS WHO SEARCHED THROUGH THEM AND POSTED EXCERPTS ON TWITTER.

MUSK AND HIS ALLIES PROMOTED THESE DOCUMENTS AS PROOF THAT TWITTER CENSORED CONSERVATIVES BECAUSE OF THEIR POLITICAL VIEWS.
MMMPH!
BUT, IF ANYTHING, THE DOCUMENTS SIMPLY SHOW THAT THE BUSINESS OF POLICING A LARGE SOCIAL NETWORK IS CHAOTICALLY DIFFICULT.
LIES
HATE
DISINFORMATION
THEY SHOW TWITTER EXECUTIVES AND RANK-AND-FILE EMPLOYEES STRUGGLING TO MAKE THE CORRECT MORAL DECISIONS, QUESTIONING THE COMPANY'S RULES, AND OCCASIONALLY GETTING THINGS WRONG.
FAKE NEWS
FOR EXAMPLE, JUST BEFORE THE 2020 PRESIDENTIAL ELECTION, TWITTER DECIDED TO BLOCK USERS FROM SHARING A *NEW YORK POST* STORY ALLEGING SHADY BUSINESS DEALINGS BY THEN-CANDIDATE JOE BIDEN'S SON, HUNTER, IN UKRAINE.
AT THE TIME, IT WASN'T AT ALL CLEAR THAT THE MATERIAL WAS AUTHENTIC, SO A PANICKED TWITTER RESTRICTED THE POST STORY.
ER... WE HAVE RULES AGAINST SHARING HACKED MATERIAL CONTAINING PRIVATE INFORMATION.
THE *NEW YORK POST*'S OWN TWITTER ACCOUNT WAS SUSPENDED UNTIL IT DELETED ITS TWEETS ABOUT THE STORY.
NEW YORK POST
!
ACCOUNT SUSPENDED

MEMORIES OF THE RUSSIAN HACK AND LEAK OF DEMOCRATIC NATIONAL COMMITTEE EMAILS IN 2016 AND ITS EFFECT ON THAT ELECTION DROVE THESE DECISIONS.
TWITTER WAS CRITICIZED FOR TAKING SUCH A HEAVY-HANDED APPROACH TO A STORY THAT WAS BEING REPORTED BY A MAJOR NEWS OUTLET.
TRUTH?
EVEN IF THAT MEDIA OUTLET WAS THE *NEW YORK POST*, WHICH AS PART OF RUPERT MURDOCH'S MEDIA EMPIRE, WAS KNOWN FOR ITS SENSATIONALISM, BLATANT ADVOCACY, AND CONSERVATIVE BIAS.
NONETHELESS, WITHIN DAYS TWITTER REVERSED THE BLOCK AND CHANGED ITS POLICIES ON HACKED MATERIALS.
THEN-CEO OF TWITTER, JACK DORSEY.
WE MADE A MISTAKE.
DESPITE ASSERTIONS BY MUSK, THE TWITTER FILES DID NOT SHOW ANY EVIDENCE THAT THERE WAS A REQUEST BY DEMOCRATS AND LAW ENFORCEMENT TO BLOCK *THE NEW YORK POST* STORY.
NOT GUILTY.
IN FACT, MUSK'S METHOD OF RELEASING THE DOCUMENTS TO FAVORED JOURNALISTS WHO THEN CHERRY-PICKED THE INFORMATION THEY WANTED, UNFAIRLY PORTRAYED THE PREVIOUS REGIME AS BIASED.

A MORE HONEST APPROACH WOULD HAVE BEEN TO RELEASE ALL THE DOCUMENTS TO ANY JOURNALIST WHO ASKED, OF WHATEVER POLITICAL PERSUASION.
BY THIS TIME ANY PRETENSE THAT MUSK WAS A CENTRIST IN HIS POLITICS WAS LONG GONE. IT WAS CLEAR FROM BOTH HIS WORDS AND ACTIONS THAT HE FAVORED THE RIGHT.
HE WROTE ON TWITTER IN DECEMBER 2022...
THE TIDE IS STARTING TO TURN ON THE MORTAL THREAT TO CIVILIZATION THAT IS THE WOKE MIND VIRUS.
BUT WOKE JUST MEANS BEING ALERT TO DISCRIMINATION AND INJUSTICE.
BLACK LIVES MATTER
FROM THIS POINT ON, TWITTER BECAME MORE FAVORABLE TO FAR-RIGHT INFLUENCERS AND ADVANCED THE INTERESTS, PREJUDICES, AND CONSPIRACY THEORIES OF THE RIGHT-WING OF AMERICAN POLITICS.
COVID-19 IS A SCAM
IF YOU WANTED TO FIND THE LATEST CONSPIRACY THEORIES TRENDING ON TWITTER, THE EASIEST THING TO DO WAS TO READ THE TWEETS ELON MUSK REPLIED TO.

OCTOBER 28, 2022, PAUL PELOSI, THE HUSBAND OF SPEAKER OF THE HOUSE OF REPRESENTATIVES NANCY PELOSI, WAS BEATEN WITH A HAMMER BY A MAN WHO BROKE INTO THE FAMILY'S HOUSE IN SAN FRANCISCO.
THIS WAS AN ACT OF POLITICALLY MOTIVATED VIOLENCE BY A MAN WHO CLAIMED HE HAD OTHERS ON HIS LIST. THE ATTACKER WAS LOOKING FOR SPEAKER PELOSI, WHO WAS NOT AT HOME.
WHERE IS NANCY?
LURID CONSPIRACY THEORIES IMMEDIATELY BEGAN TO BE CIRCULATED BY RIGHT-WING COMMENTATORS.
LIES
HATE
MUSK CONTRIBUTED TO THIS BY TWEETING THAT "THERE MIGHT BE MORE TO THIS STORY." HE POSTED A SCREENSHOT OF A SPURIOUS REPORT ACCUSING MR. PELOSI OF GETTING INTO A DRUNKEN FIGHT WITH A MALE PROSTITUTE.
SEND
HE SOON DELETED THIS TWEET, BUT TENS OF THOUSANDS OF PEOPLE HAD ALREADY SEEN AND SHARED IT...
...AMPLIFYING THE LIE, RATHER THAN THE TRUTH.
FAKE NEWS

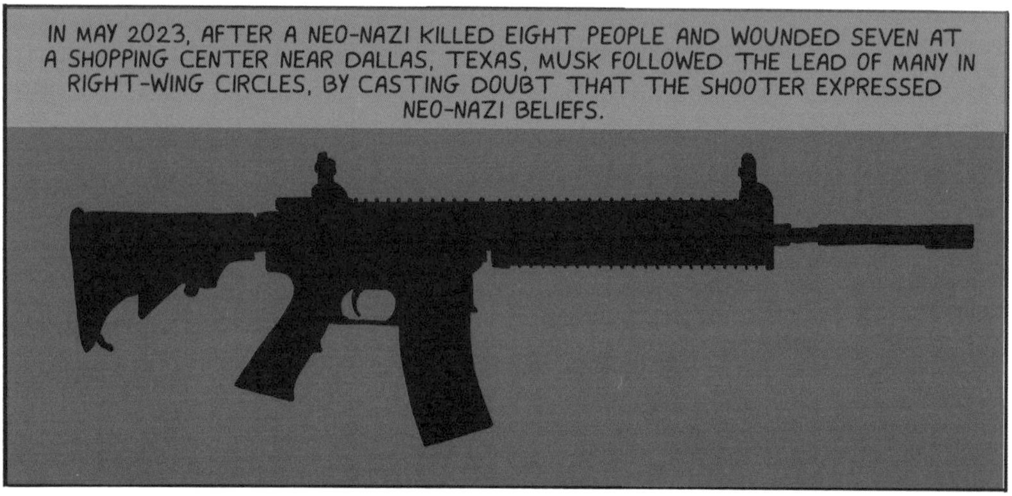
IN MAY 2023, AFTER A NEO-NAZI KILLED EIGHT PEOPLE AND WOUNDED SEVEN AT A SHOPPING CENTER NEAR DALLAS, TEXAS, MUSK FOLLOWED THE LEAD OF MANY IN RIGHT-WING CIRCLES, BY CASTING DOUBT THAT THE SHOOTER EXPRESSED NEO-NAZI BELIEFS.

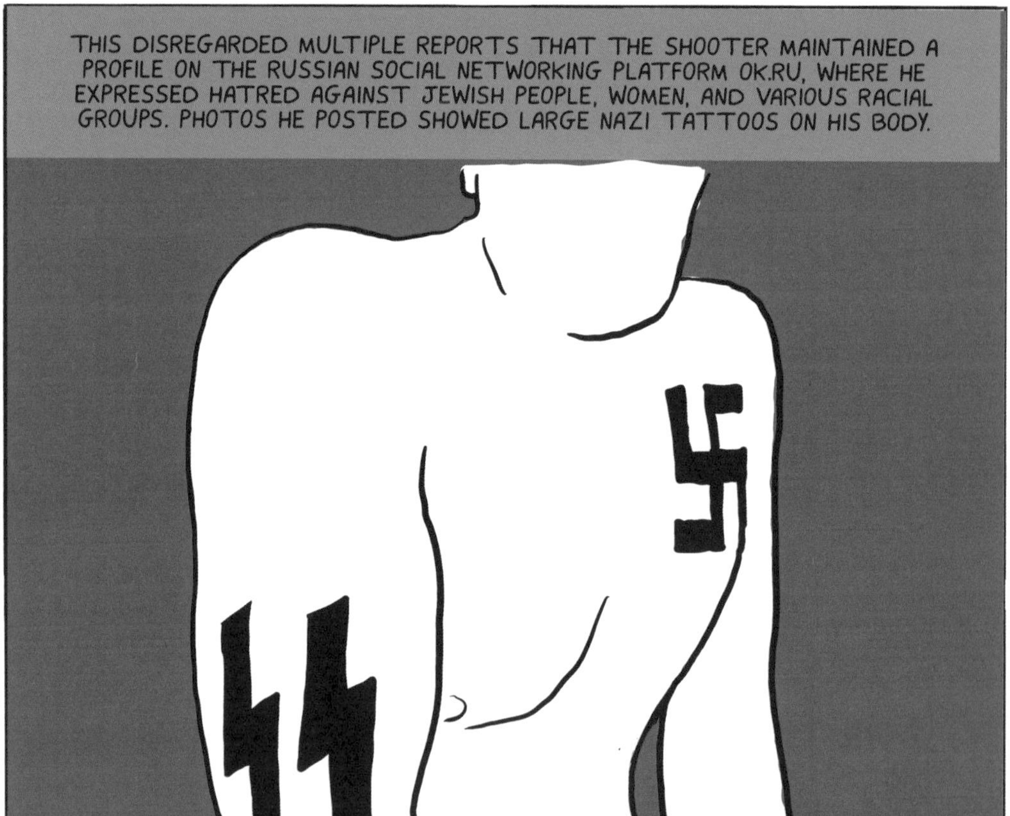
THIS DISREGARDED MULTIPLE REPORTS THAT THE SHOOTER MAINTAINED A PROFILE ON THE RUSSIAN SOCIAL NETWORKING PLATFORM OK.RU, WHERE HE EXPRESSED HATRED AGAINST JEWISH PEOPLE, WOMEN, AND VARIOUS RACIAL GROUPS. PHOTOS HE POSTED SHOWED LARGE NAZI TATTOOS ON HIS BODY.
MUSK REACTED TO A SERIES OF TWEETS SUGGESTING THAT THE REPORTING OF THE SHOOTER'S RIGHT-WING MOTIVES WERE "SUSPECT" AND THAT THE ATTACK WAS "A PSYOP" (A MILITARY OPERATION PERFORMED BY A UNIT SPECIALIZING IN PSYCHOLOGICAL WARFARE). HE OFFERED NO EVIDENCE TO SUPPORT THIS.

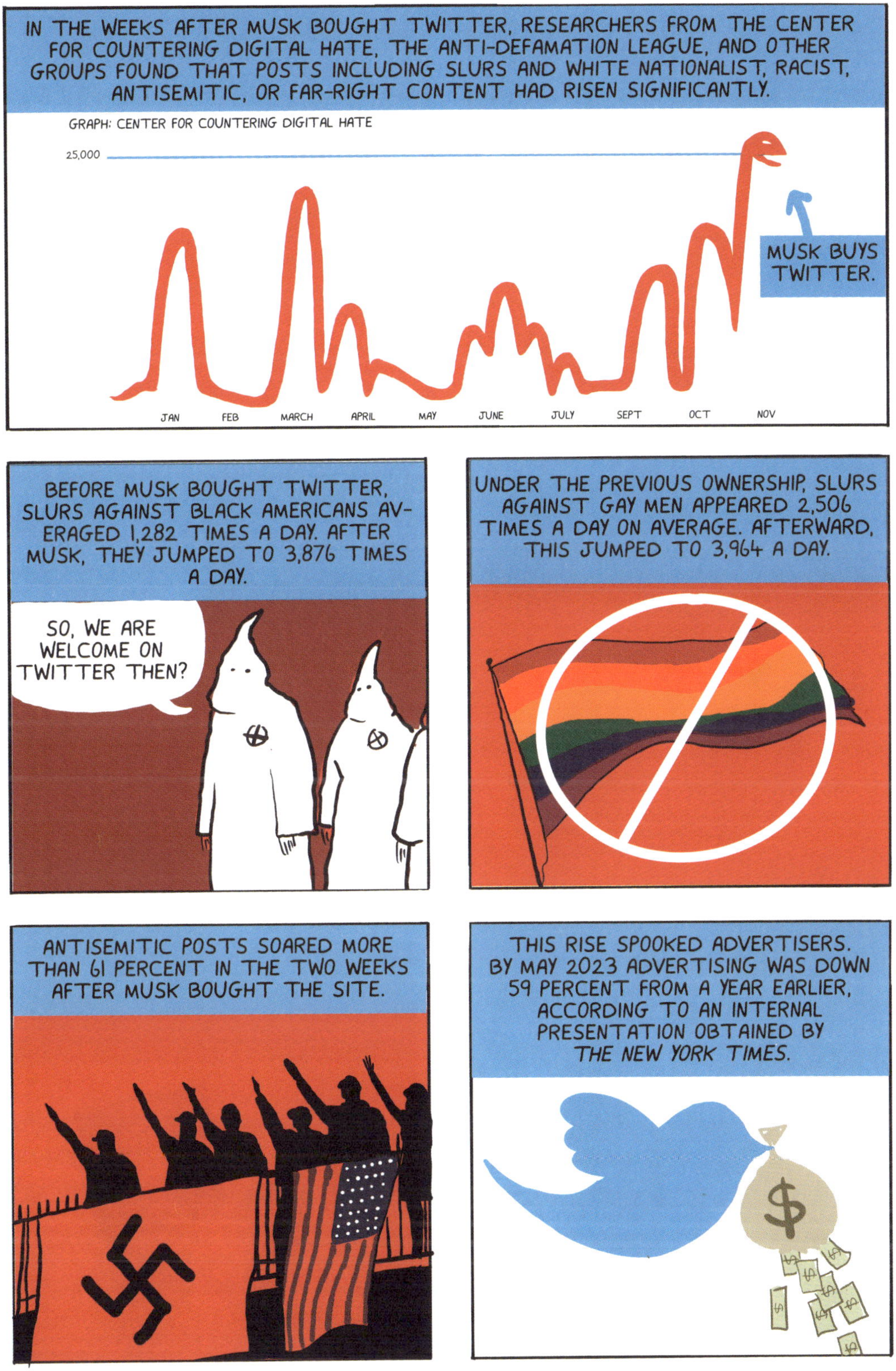
IN THE WEEKS AFTER MUSK BOUGHT TWITTER, RESEARCHERS FROM THE CENTER FOR COUNTERING DIGITAL HATE, THE ANTI-DEFAMATION LEAGUE, AND OTHER GROUPS FOUND THAT POSTS INCLUDING SLURS AND WHITE NATIONALIST, RACIST, ANTISEMITIC, OR FAR-RIGHT CONTENT HAD RISEN SIGNIFICANTLY.
GRAPH: CENTER FOR COUNTERING DIGITAL HATE
25,000
MUSK BUYS TWITTER.
JAN
FEB
MARCH
APRIL
MAY
JUNE
JULY
SEPT
OCT
NOV
BEFORE MUSK BOUGHT TWITTER, SLURS AGAINST BLACK AMERICANS AVERAGED 1,282 TIMES A DAY. AFTER MUSK, THEY JUMPED TO 3,876 TIMES A DAY.
SO, WE ARE WELCOME ON TWITTER THEN?
UNDER THE PREVIOUS OWNERSHIP, SLURS AGAINST GAY MEN APPEARED 2,506 TIMES A DAY ON AVERAGE. AFTERWARD, THIS JUMPED TO 3,964 A DAY.
ANTISEMITIC POSTS SOARED MORE THAN 61 PERCENT IN THE TWO WEEKS AFTER MUSK BOUGHT THE SITE.
THIS RISE SPOOKED ADVERTISERS. BY MAY 2023 ADVERTISING WAS DOWN 59 PERCENT FROM A YEAR EARLIER, ACCORDING TO AN INTERNAL PRESENTATION OBTAINED BY *THE NEW YORK TIMES*.

FROM THE BEGINNING, MUSK DIDN'T SEEM THAT INVESTED IN RUNNING TWITTER WELL. HE APPEARED MORE INTERESTED IN USING THE SITE TO DIMINISH THE POLITICAL LEFT'S INFLUENCE AND PUSH A RIGHT-WING WORLDVIEW.
MAGA
IN APRIL 2023, TWITTER ADDED A WARNING TO NATIONAL PUBLIC RADIO'S (NPR) TWITTER ACCOUNT LABELING IT AS "US STATE-AFFILIATED MEDIA."
WAIT, WAIT.
NPR
THAT'S A LABEL USUALLY GIVEN TO STATE-CONTROLLED PROPAGANDA OUTLETS, SUCH AS RUSSIA TODAY (RT), AND CHINA'S XINHUA.
NPR
THIS PLEASED NPR'S RIGHT-WING CRITICS, WHO HAVE LONG CLAIMED THAT THE RADIO STATION HAD A LIBERAL BIAS.
WE'RE AN INDEPENDENT NONPROFIT NOT AFFILIATED WITH THE US GOVERNMENT.
NPR
NPR NO LONGER MAINTAINS ITS TWITTER ACCOUNT IN A DIRECT RESPONSE TO TWITTER'S LABELING OF THE OUTLET.
WHERE ARE YOU GOING?
NPR
TWITTER ADDED THE SAME LABEL TO THE PUBLIC BROADCASTING SERVICE (PBS), THE BRITISH BROADCASTING CORPORATION (BBC), AND VOICE OF AMERICA (VOA).
BBC
STATE-AFFILIATED
PBS

LIKE MANY OF MUSK'S TWITTER DECISIONS, THIS POLICY APPEARS TO HAVE BEEN MADE WITHOUT ANY REAL THOUGHT. IT WAS DONE ON A WHIM AS PART OF A PATTERN OF DECISIONS MEANT TO FAVOR THE POLITICAL RIGHT.
TRUTH
WITHIN WEEKS HE REVERSED THE LABELING POLICY ENTIRELY, ENDING THE PRACTICE EVEN ON MEDIA OUTLETS THAT ACTUALLY WERE PROPAGANDA OUTLETS FOR THEIR GOVERNMENTS.
TRUTH
GOOD NEWS FOR AUTHORITARIAN REGIMES WANTING TO SPREAD DISINFORMATION.
ON MAY 12, 2023, AHEAD OF AN ELECTION IN TURKEY, TWITTER BOWED TO THE DEMANDS OF AUTHORITARIAN TURKISH PRESIDENT RECEP TAYYIP ERDOGAN AND RESTRICTED ACCESS TO SOME CONTENT IN THAT COUNTRY.
REPORTS FROM TURKEY INDICATED THAT IT WAS ERDOGAN'S POLITICAL OPPONENTS AND JOURNALISTS WHO'D BEEN CRITICAL OF HIM THAT WERE BEING SUPPRESSED.
IN HIS DEFENSE, MUSK CLAIMED THAT THE CAPITULATION WAS MEANT TO KEEP TWITTER FROM BEING BLOCKED FROM TURKEY IN ITS ENTIRETY.
ERDOGAN

COMPARE MUSK'S EASY CAPITULATION WITH OTHER INTERNET COMPANIES, WHO WERE FACED WITH BANS AND FOUGHT HARD FOR FREE SPEECH.
AFTER WIKIPEDIA WAS BANNED IN TURKEY, THE COMPANY TOOK THE GOVERNMENT TO COURT AND WON AFTER A TWO-YEAR LEGAL BATTLE IN 2019.
BLOCKED
WE STOOD STRONG FOR OUR PRINCIPLES AND TOOK OUR FIGHT TO THE SUPREME COURT OF TURKEY AND WON. THIS IS WHAT IT MEANS TO TREAT FREEDOM OF EXPRESSION AS A PRINCIPLE RATHER THAN A SLOGAN.
WIKIPEDIA COFOUNDER, JIMMY WALES
PRIOR TO MUSK'S OWNERSHIP, IN 2014, TWITTER HAD CHALLENGED A TURKISH BAN AND WON THE CASE IN TWO DAYS.
MUSK HAS HAD STRONG BUSINESS CONNECTIONS IN TURKEY SINCE AT LEAST 2017, WHEN HE MET ERDOGAN...
AND THE TWO MEN DISCUSSED JOINT OPERATIONS BETWEEN TESLA, SPACEX, AND TURKISH FIRMS, AS WELL AS THE LAUNCH OF TURKEY'S TURKSAT 5A AND 5B SATELLITES.

MMM. IT'S ALMOST AS IF MUSK ONLY BELIEVES IN FREE SPEECH WHEN IT DOESN'T AFFECT HIS BUSINESS INTERESTS.
IN DECEMBER 2022, MUSK ASKED TWITTER USERS WHETHER HE SHOULD STEP DOWN AS THE HEAD OF THE COMPANY, PROMISING TO ABIDE BY THE RESULTS OF THE POLL.
SHOULD I STAY OR SHOULD I GO?
THE RESULTS OF THE SURVEY, WHICH LASTED TWELVE HOURS, SHOWED THAT THE MAJORITY OF THOSE WHO VOTED (57. 5 PERCENT) WANTED HIM TO LEAVE.
GO.
FIVE MONTHS LATER IT WAS ANNOUNCED THAT MUSK'S REPLACEMENT AS CEO OF TWITTER WOULD BE LINDA YACCARINO, WHO'D PREVIOUSLY BEEN NBCUNIVERSAL'S HEAD OF GLOBAL ADVERTISING.
HI!
MUSK STATED THAT YACCARINO WOULD FOCUS ON BUSINESS OPERATIONS WHILE HE WOULD CONCENTRATE ON PRODUCT DESIGN AND NEW TECHNOLOGY. HIS NEW JOB TITLE WAS EXECUTIVE CHAIR.
I'M GOING TO BRING TOP COMPANIES BACK TO TWITTER, EVEN THOUGH IN MY PREVIOUS JOB I SPENT YEARS SAYING SOCIAL MEDIA PLATFORMS ARE TOO UNSTABLE FOR BLUE-CHIP BRANDS.

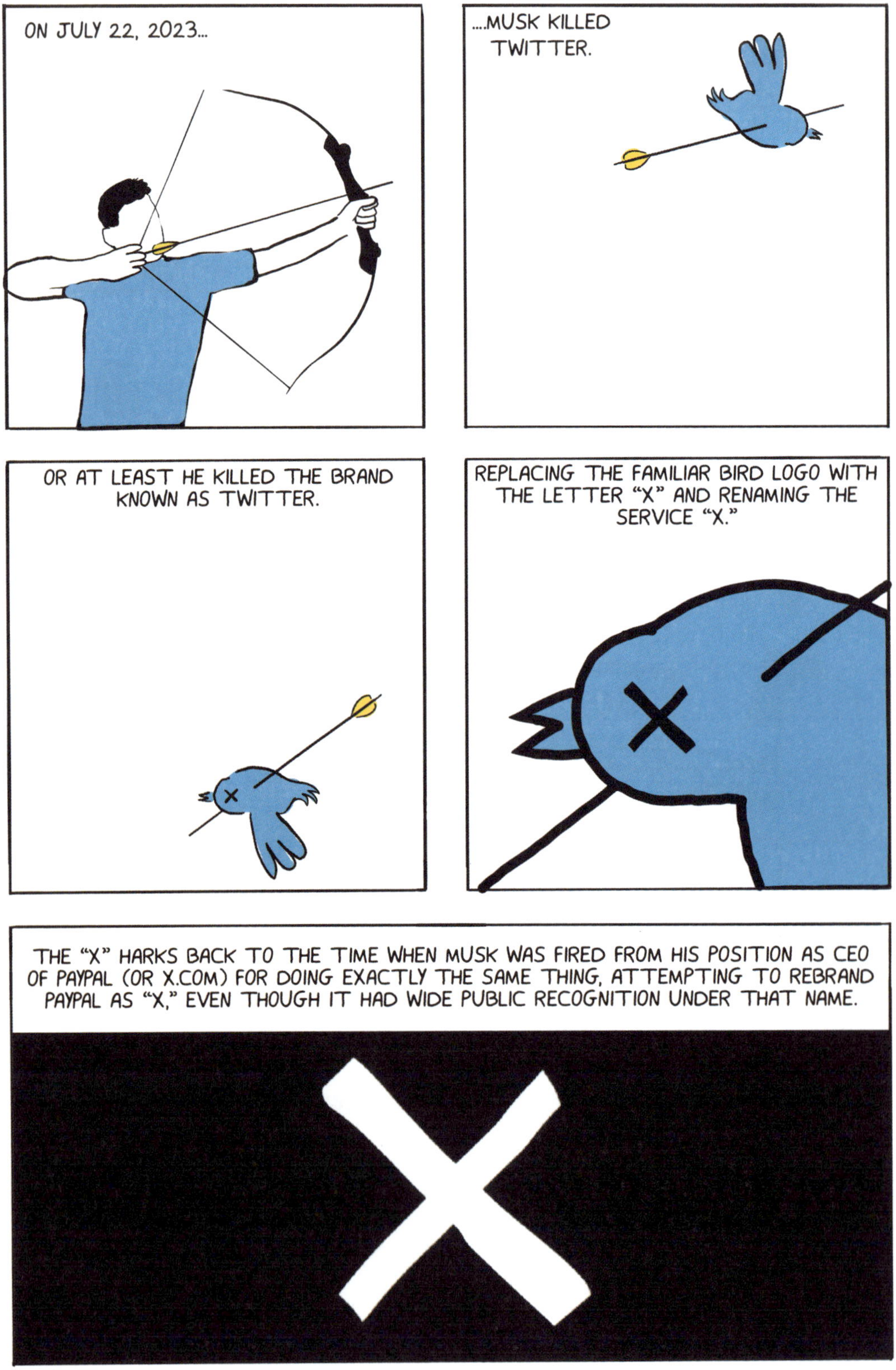
ON JULY 22, 2023...
....MUSK KILLED TWITTER.
OR AT LEAST HE KILLED THE BRAND KNOWN AS TWITTER.
REPLACING THE FAMILIAR BIRD LOGO WITH THE LETTER "X" AND RENAMING THE SERVICE "X."
THE "X" HARKS BACK TO THE TIME WHEN MUSK WAS FIRED FROM HIS POSITION AS CEO OF PAYPAL (OR X.COM) FOR DOING EXACTLY THE SAME THING, ATTEMPTING TO REBRAND PAYPAL AS "X," EVEN THOUGH IT HAD WIDE PUBLIC RECOGNITION UNDER THAT NAME.

MUSK HAS SAID THAT HIS EVENTUAL AIM IS TO USE "X" AS THE BASIS FOR AN "EVERYTHING APP."
MUCH LIKE THE CHINESE INSTANT-MESSAGING, SOCIAL MEDIA, AND MOBILE PAYMENT APP KNOWN AS WECHAT...
...USED TO BUY GROCERIES, BOOK DOCTOR'S APPOINTMENTS, SHARE PHOTOS WITH FRIENDS, PLAY GAMES, AND NUMEROUS OTHER THINGS.
WHICH IS ESSENTIALLY WHAT HE WAS ATTEMPTING TO DO IN 2000 WITH X.COM. IT'S AS IF HE'S TRYING TO RECTIFY A DECADES-OLD GRIEVANCE.
IT'S AS IF HE WANTS TO PROVE THAT THE IDEA THAT GOT HIM EJECTED FROM PAYPAL WILL WORK, DESPITE THE MOVE WIPING OUT TWITTER'S BRAND VALUE.
MERCURIAL DECISIONS BASED ON WHIMS, OFTEN SOON WALKED BACK, HAVE BEEN MUSK'S BUSINESS STRATEGY IN RECENT YEARS.

ON JULY 28, THE RENAMED COMPANY ERECTED A GIANT PULSING AND STROBING "X" LOGO ON THE ROOF OF ITS MARKET STREET HEADQUARTERS IN SAN FRANCISCO. RESIDENTS IN THE AREA COMPLAINED ABOUT THE INTRUSIVE LIGHT POLLUTION.
THE SIGN WAS BUILT WITHOUT A PERMIT. CITY BUILDING INSPECTORS WERE TWICE DENIED ACCESS TO THE ROOF. THE SIGN REMAINED THERE FOR A WEEKEND, BUT ON MONDAY, JULY 31, IT WAS DISMANTLED.

MEANWHILE, BACK AT MUSK'S CORE BUSINESS, TESLA RELEASED THE MODEL Y, AN ALL-ELECTRIC FAMILY SUV IN 2020. SMALLER AND LESS EXPENSIVE THAN THE MODEL X, IT SHARED AN ESTIMATED 75 PERCENT OF ITS PARTS WITH THE TESLA MODEL 3.
TESLA THEN RELEASED THE TESLA SEMI, A BATTERY-ELECTRIC CLASS 8 SEMI-TRUCK, POWERED BY THREE CARBON-FIBER-WRAPPED MOTORS.
THE FIRST CUSTOMER FOR THE SEMI WAS PEPSICO, WHO BEGAN ADDING THE TRUCKS TO THEIR PEPSI BEVERAGE AND FRITO-LAY SNACK FOOD TRANSPORTATION FLEETS IN LATE 2022.
THEN CAME THE TESLA CYBERTRUCK, A BATTERY-ELECTRIC LIGHT-DUTY TRUCK, ANNOUNCED IN NOVEMBER 2019. MASS PRODUCTION BEGAN IN LATE 2023.
AT THE UNVEILING OF THE CYBERTRUCK, TESLA'S LEAD DESIGNER FRANZ VON HOLZHAUSEN BROKE TWO OF THE TRUCK'S WINDOWS WITH A METAL BALL IN A FAILED ATTEMPT TO SHOW JUST HOW UNBREAKABLE THE WINDOWS WERE.
OOPS!

IN DECEMBER 2023, TESLA CONFIRMED THAT THE CYBERTRUCK WILL ONLY BE AVAILABLE IN THE UNITED STATES, CANADA, AND MEXICO. THERE ARE NO PLANS TO RELEASE IT IN OTHER GLOBAL MARKETS.

THE MAIN REASON THE CYBERTRUCK MAY NEVER BE SOLD IN EUROPE IS TOUGH EU SAFETY RULES AIMED AT PROTECTING PEDESTRIANS BY LIMITING EXTERNAL PROTRUSIONS. IN EUROPE, A VEHICLE OF CYBERTRUCK'S SIZE, POWER, AND WEIGHT MAY BE SEEN AS LETHAL TO PEDESTRIANS AND CYCLISTS. AMERICAN RULES ON THE SIZE OF VEHICLES ARE FAR LAXER, AND THIS HAS LED TO EVER-LARGER CARS AND TRUCKS CAUSING A SAFETY CRISIS ON US STREETS. SINCE 2010, PEDESTRIAN DEATHS IN THE US HAVE CLIMBED A SHOCKING 77 PERCENT. THE CYBERTRUCK IS UNLIKELY TO BRING THIS FIGURE DOWN.

BUT EVEN IN THE US THE CYBERTRUCK MAY NOT FARE WELL. THE TRUCK MARKET IS GOVERNED MORE BY PRACTICAL DEMANDS THAN FUTURISTIC AESTHETICS. THE VEHICLE IS LIKELY TO END UP BEING NO MORE THAN A NICHE NOVELTY ITEM.

CONSTANTLY DELAYED IS THE SECOND-GENERATION TESLA ROADSTER. A FOUR-SEATER COUPE WITH A REMOVABLE GLASS ROOF, WHICH MUSK INITIALLY CLAIMED WILL BE CAPABLE OF ACCELERATING FROM ZERO TO 60 MPH IN 1.9 SECONDS. THE CAR WAS ANNOUNCED WAY BACK IN 2017.

UNDER DEVELOPMENT AT SPACEX IS STARSHIP, WHICH, STACKED ON TOP OF ITS BOOSTER, IS DESIGNED TO TRANSPORT CREW AND CARGO TO A VARIETY OF DESTINATIONS, INCLUDING EARTH'S ORBIT, THE MOON, MARS, AND BEYOND. SPACEX CLAIMS THAT STARSHIP WILL BE ABLE TO CARRY UP TO ONE HUNDRED PEOPLE ON LONG-DURATION INTERPLANETARY FLIGHTS.

NASA'S SATURN V, WHICH TOOK ASTRONAUTS TO THE MOON IN THE 1960S AND '70S AS PART OF THE APOLLO PROGRAM.
SPACEX STARSHIP. 120 METERS (394 FEET) IN HEIGHT.
STATUE OF LIBERTY.
USA
ON APRIL 20, 2023, STARSHIP WAS LAUNCHED AT SPACEX STARBASE IN BOCA CHICA, TEXAS, ON ITS FIRST ORBITAL TEST FLIGHT...
BUT ABOUT FOUR MINUTES AFTER LIFTOFF, THE ROCKET EXPLODED WITHOUT REACHING ORBIT, WHEN THE SUPER HEAVY BOOSTER AND STARSHIP WERE UNABLE TO DISENTANGLE THEMSELVES.

THIS WAS NOT THE ONLY DAMAGE DONE. THE COLOSSAL FORCES NEEDED TO BLAST THE ROCKET INTO THE AIR, BLEW UP THE LAUNCH PAD...
AND HURLED CHUNKS OF CONCRETE AND METAL THOUSANDS OF FEET INTO A SENSITIVE WILDLIFE HABITAT AND IGNITED A 3.5-ACRE FIRE ON NEARBY STATE PARK LAND.
ASH AND SAND-LIKE PARTICULATE MATTER RAINED DOWN ON PORT ISABEL, A TOWN ABOUT SIX MILES FROM THE LAUNCHPAD, AND SOUTH PADRE ISLAND, A FEW MILES UP THE COAST.
FIVE ENVIRONMENTAL AND CULTURAL HERITAGE GROUPS SUED THE FEDERAL AVIATION ADMINISTRATION, ALLEGING THAT THE AGENCY VIOLATED THE NATIONAL ENVIRONMENT POLICY ACT WHEN IT ALLOWED SPACEX TO LAUNCH THE ROCKET WITHOUT A COMPREHENSIVE ENVIRONMENTAL REVIEW.

IN 2021, NASA SELECTED STARSHIP TO BE THE FIRST CREWED LUNAR LANDER FOR ITS ARTEMIS PROGRAM OF MOON EXPLORATION, INTENDED TO PUT ASTRONAUTS DOWN NEAR THE ICE-RICH LUNAR SOUTH POLE, IN HUMANITY'S FIRST RETURN TO THE MOON SINCE THE APOLLO PROGRAM ENDED IN 1972. LAUNCH DATE DECEMBER 2026.

THE FEDERAL AVIATION ADMINISTRATION INVESTIGATION INTO THE LAUNCH MISHAP CONCLUDED THAT SPACEX MUST TAKE CORRECTIVE ACTIONS, INCLUDING REDESIGNS OF VEHICLE HARDWARE, REDESIGN OF THE LAUNCH PAD TO INCREASE ITS ROBUSTNESS, INCORPORATION OF ADDITIONAL REVIEWS IN THE DESIGN PROCESS, ADDITIONAL ANALYSIS AND TESTING OF SAFETY CRITICAL SYSTEMS, AND THE APPLICATION OF ADDITIONAL CHANGE CONTROL PRACTICES. A FURTHER FLIGHT WAS ATTEMPTED IN MARCH 2024, WHEN STARSHIP SUCCESSFULLY FLEW HALFWAY AROUND THE GLOBE, BUT CONTACT WAS LOST DURING THE FINAL STAGES OF THE TEST. IT EITHER BURNED UP OR CAME APART DURING REENTRY.

ELON MUSK HAS DREAMT OF MAKING HUMANS A MULTIPLANETARY SPECIES SINCE HE WAS VERY YOUNG. COLONIZATION OF MARS HAS BEEN A MAJOR GOAL OF SPACEX SINCE ITS FOUNDING TWO DECADES AGO. IN APRIL 2021, AFTER SPACEX WON A $2.9 BILLION CONTRACT FROM NASA, HE SAID...
IT'S BEEN NOW ALMOST HALF A CENTURY SINCE HUMANS WERE LAST ON THE MOON. THAT'S TOO LONG.
WE NEED TO GET BACK THERE AND HAVE A PERMANENT BASE ON THE MOON — AGAIN, LIKE A BIG PERMANENTLY OCCUPIED BASE ON THE MOON.
AND THEN BUILD A CITY ON MARS TO BECOME A SPACEFARING CIVILIZATION, A MULTI-PLANET SPECIES.
AT THE TIME OF WRITING MUSK IS WORTH $324.3 BILLION.
IS ACHIEVING SUCH WEALTH PROOF THAT HE'S THE SMARTEST MAN IN THE WORLD?
IN MUSK WE TRUST.
MUSK FAN.

BECAUSE HOW ELSE COULD ANYONE ACHIEVE SUCH WEALTH UNLESS THEY WERE PHENOMENALLY TALENTED AND INTELLIGENT? IT GOES WITHOUT SAYING. LOOK AT ALL THAT HE'S INVENTED.
BUT IS THIS TRUE? MUSK UNDOUBTEDLY HAS GREAT DRIVE, RUTHLESSNESS, AND A FACILITY FOR CONSTANT SELF-PROMOTION, BUT HE'S NOT AN INVENTOR, AND HE'S CERTAINLY NOT A SCIENTIST.
THAT'S NONSENSE.
MUSK CAME FROM A PLACE OF PRIVILEGE. SIMPLY BY BEING BORN FINANCIALLY WELL-OFF AND WHITE IN SOUTH AFRICA DURING APARTHEID GAVE HIM AN ADVANTAGE THE GREAT MASS OF HIS FELLOW COUNTRYMEN DID NOT HAVE. WOULD THE WORLD EVER HAVE HEARD OF HIM IF HE'D BEEN BORN BLACK?
DANGER
NATIVES: INDIANS & COLOUREDS.
IF YOU ENTER THESE PREMISES AT NIGHT, YOU WILL BE LISTED AS MISSING.
ARMED GUARDS SHOOT ON SIGHT. SAVAGE DOGS DEVOUR THE CORPSE.
YOU HAVE BEEN WARNED!
CREDIT IS DUE TO HIM FOR MAKING THE MOST OF THE DIFFICULT SITUATION OF HIS EARLY LIFE, BUT HE STILL HAD ACCESS TO ELITE EDUCATION...
...AND A WAY OUT OF THE STULTIFYING CULTURE OF SOUTH AFRICA, DENIED TO MILLIONS OF OTHERS.

THE GENERAL PUBLIC, MUSK'S FANS, AND A CREDULOUS MEDIA CREDIT THE BILLIONAIRE WITH GENIUS. THEY SEE SPACEX AND TESLA'S ACHIEVEMENTS AND THINK THAT HE ALONE HAS BUILT THESE COMPANIES. BUT EVEN A CURSORY READING OF THE HISTORY OF THESE COMPANIES WILL GIVE YOU THE NAMES OF PEOPLE WHO SHOULD GET AS MUCH CREDIT AS MUSK, IF NOT MORE.
MARTIN EBERHARD AND MARC TARPENNING. TESLA FOUNDERS.
J.B STRAUBEL. TESLA FOUNDER AND FORMER CHIEF TECHNICAL OFFICER.
FRANZ VON HOLZHAUSEN. TESLA CHIEF DESIGNER.
TOM MUELLER. SPACEX ROCKET-ENGINE DESIGNER.
AND HUNDREDS OF OTHERS WHO ARE ESSENTIAL TO MUSK'S SUCCESS BUT WHO GET LITTLE CREDIT BECAUSE THE MYTH OF A SELF-MADE BILLIONAIRE IS A FAR MORE ATTRACTIVE STORY THAN THE MORE MUNDANE TRUTH.

IN JANUARY 2024, THE WALL STREET JOURNAL PUBLISHED A DETAILED ARTICLE ABOUT ELON MUSK'S DRUG USE, STATING THAT THIS HABIT HAD BEEN OF INTEREST TO THE MEMBERS OF TESLA'S BOARD FOR YEARS, TO SUCH AN EXTENT THAT THEY HAD DISCUSSED ELON'S BEHAVIOR WITH KIMBAL, ELON'S BROTHER, WHO SITS ON THE BOARDS OF TESLA AND SPACEX.
DRUGS
THE WALL STREET JOURNAL WENT ON TO CLAIM IN ANOTHER ARTICLE THAT MUSK HAS ALSO TAKEN DRUGS WITH EXECUTIVES AT HIS COMPANIES AS WELL AS DRUGS WITH AN UNNAMED SPACEX BOARD MEMBER. MUSK HAS DENIED THESE ALLEGATIONS.
SIMPLY NOT TRUE.
ACCORDING TO THE NEWSPAPER, MUSK'S DRUG CONSUMPTION AND VOLATILE BEHAVIOR PUSHED FORMER TESLA DIRECTOR LINDA JOHNSON RICE NOT TO RUN FOR REELECTION TO TESLA'S EXECUTIVE BOARD IN 2019. MUSK HAS DENIED THESE CLAIMS AND STATED THAT HER DEPARTURE WAS AMICABLE AND SHE SIMPLY CAME TO THE END OF HER TERM.
GOODBYE.
DURING A RECORDING SESSION OF THE 'JOE ROGAN EXPERIENCE' PODCAST IN 2018, MUSK SMOKED MARIJUANA ON VIDEO.
THIS EVENT STRAINED HIS RELATIONSHIP WITH NASA, WHO DEMANDED ASSURANCES THAT SPACEX WAS A DRUG-FREE WORKPLACE.
OCCU

A JANUARY 2024 FORBES ARTICLE REPORTED THAT MUSK HAD ALLEGEDLY AGREED TO UNDERGO RANDOM DRUG TESTING FOR THREE YEARS AFTER HIS APPEARANCE ON THE PODCAST. HE CLAIMED THAT DURING THIS TIME "NOT EVEN TRACE QUANTITIES" OF DRUGS OR ALCOHOL WERE FOUND IN HIS BODY.
UNNAMED SOURCES QUOTED IN AN EARLIER ARTICLE IN THE WALL STREET JOURNAL SAY THAT MUSK TAKES KETAMINE IN MICRODOSES TO TREAT DEPRESSION AND USES HIGHER DOSES OF THE DRUG AT SOCIAL EVENTS.
MUSK ADMITTED TO TAKING KETAMINE TO TREAT DEPRESSION AND RAILED AGAINST "ZOMBIFYING PEOPLE WITH SSRIs," REFERRING TO SELECTIVE SEROTONIN REUPTAKE INHIBITORS, THE MOST COMMONLY PRESCRIBED CLASS OF DRUG PRESCRIBED FOR THE MENTAL ILLNESS.
SSRIs DO HAVE SIDE EFFECTS, BUT AN INCAPACITY TO THINK ISN'T ONE OF THEM.
THE US FOOD AND DRUG ADMINISTRATION APPROVED AN INHALABLE VERSION OF A KETAMINE-DERIVED DRUG FOR TREATMENT-RESISTANT DEPRESSION IN 2019, BUT RECREATIONAL USE OF KETAMINE IS STILL ILLEGAL.
QUOTE FROM WALTER ISAACSON's BIOGRAPHY OF MUSK.
I REALLY DON'T LIKE DOING ILLEGAL DRUGS.

MUSK IS BRILLIANT IN CERTAIN LIMITED AREAS, BUT HAS A TENDENCY TOWARDS UNTHINKING RASHNESS. HE IS SKILLED AT RAKING IN PUBLIC MONEY. NEITHER TESLA NOR SPACEX WOULD EXIST WITHOUT INJECTIONS OF US TAXPAYERS' CASH. TESLA ONLY EXISTS BECAUSE OF GOVERNMENT SUBSIDIES AND TAX BREAKS, COMBINED WITH SELLING CARBON CREDIT TO ACHIEVE PROFITABILITY. NASA ESSENTIALLY FUNDS SPACEX. THERE WOULD BE NO MUSK FORTUNE WITHOUT US TAXPAYER BACKING.

MUSK HAS USED THIS FORTUNE TO DISTORT AND DEGRADE PUBLIC DISCOURSE. THE OLD VERSION OF TWITTER WAS FAR FROM A PERFECT PLATFORM, BUT IT BROKE NEWS FASTER THAN ANY OTHER SOCIAL MEDIA OR NEWS SITE AND THE DIRECT GLOBAL COMMUNICATION IT OFFERED FOR JOURNALISTS AND ACTIVISTS WAS UNPARALLELED. NOW THAT FUNCTION HAS BEEN COMPROMISED.

SINCE MUSK'S ACQUISITION, TWITTER (OR X) HAS BECOME A PLACE THAT FAVORS THE INTERESTS, PREJUDICES, AND CONSPIRACY THEORIES OF THE RIGHT-WING OF AMERICAN POLITICS, AND THIS BIAS HAS UNLEASHED A TIDE OF RACISM, ANTISEMITISM, CLIMATE DENIAL, ANTI-LGBTQ+ HATE, AND HEALTH MISINFORMATION ACROSS THE SITE.
LIES

THE FAR RIGHT FOUND THEMSELVES UNABLE TO CREATE A SUCCESSFUL SOCIAL MEDIA PLATFORM, SO MUSK "INNOVATED" BY BUYING TWITTER AND ALLOWING IT TO BECOME THE DANGEROUS AND HATEFUL FREE-FOR-ALL THAT CONSERVATIVES SEE AS ESSENTIAL IF THEY ARE TO WIN AND KEEP POWER.
TRUTH

THE US GOVERNMENT HAS EFFECTIVELY HANDED OVER STATE CAPACITY TO MUSK AS A MILITARY CONTRACTOR AND HAS THEN BEEN SURPRISED THAT HE'S STARTED TO DICTATE POLICY. HE HAS DIRECTLY INTERFERED IN UKRAINE'S ATTEMPTS TO RESIST THE RUSSIAN INVASION OF THEIR COUNTRY. IN 2023, ELON MUSK REFUSED A REQUEST BY THE UKRAINIANS TO USE HIS STARLINK SATELLITE COMMUNICATIONS NETWORK IN A DRONE-SUB ATTACK ON RUSSIAN WARSHIPS.
BELARUS
RUSSIA
POLAND
KIEV
UKRAINE
SLOVAKIA
MOLDOVA
HUNGARY
ROMANIA
SERBIA

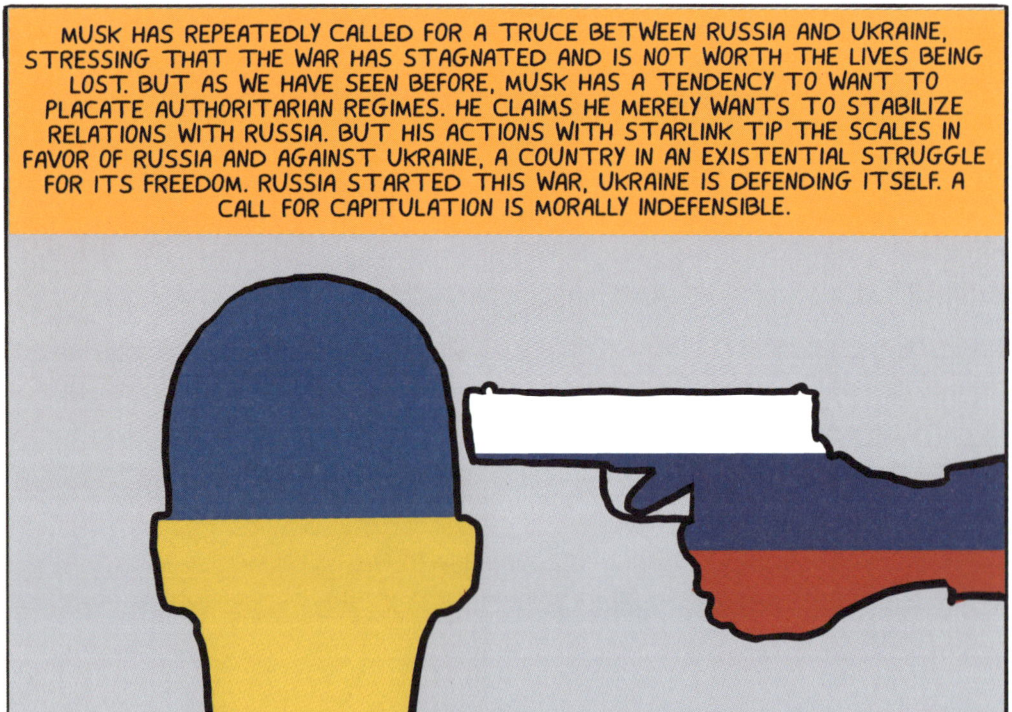
MUSK HAS REPEATEDLY CALLED FOR A TRUCE BETWEEN RUSSIA AND UKRAINE, STRESSING THAT THE WAR HAS STAGNATED AND IS NOT WORTH THE LIVES BEING LOST. BUT AS WE HAVE SEEN BEFORE, MUSK HAS A TENDENCY TO WANT TO PLACATE AUTHORITARIAN REGIMES. HE CLAIMS HE MERELY WANTS TO STABILIZE RELATIONS WITH RUSSIA. BUT HIS ACTIONS WITH STARLINK TIP THE SCALES IN FAVOR OF RUSSIA AND AGAINST UKRAINE, A COUNTRY IN AN EXISTENTIAL STRUGGLE FOR ITS FREEDOM. RUSSIA STARTED THIS WAR, UKRAINE IS DEFENDING ITSELF. A CALL FOR CAPITULATION IS MORALLY INDEFENSIBLE.

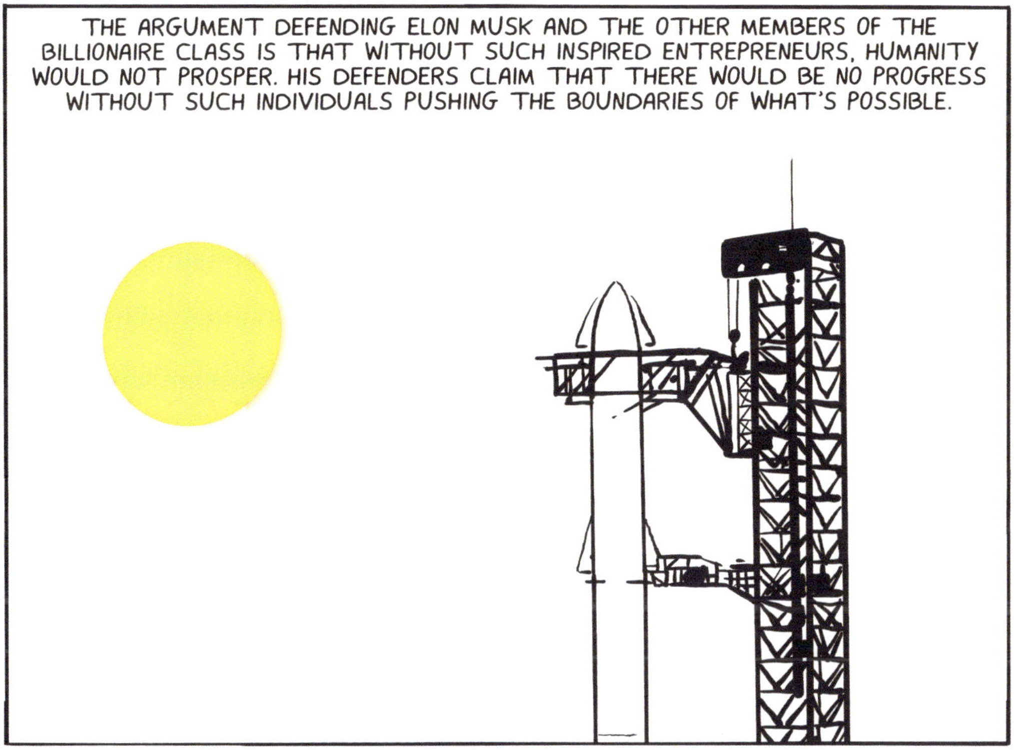
THE ARGUMENT DEFENDING ELON MUSK AND THE OTHER MEMBERS OF THE BILLIONAIRE CLASS IS THAT WITHOUT SUCH INSPIRED ENTREPRENEURS, HUMANITY WOULD NOT PROSPER. HIS DEFENDERS CLAIM THAT THERE WOULD BE NO PROGRESS WITHOUT SUCH INDIVIDUALS PUSHING THE BOUNDARIES OF WHAT'S POSSIBLE.

BUT IN A PREVIOUS ERA, MANKIND REACHED SPACE AND LANDED ON THE MOON WITHOUT THE LEADERSHIP OF THE EXTREMELY RICH. SPACEX ONLY EXISTS BECAUSE OF A US GOVERNMENT POLICY DECISION TO DIVERT FUNDS INTO THE PRIVATE SECTOR. ELON MUSK RODE THE WAVE OF TECHNOLOGICAL ADVANCEMENT AND TOOK ADVANTAGE OF LUCRATIVE GOVERNMENT CONTRACTS AND HISTORICALLY LOW TAXATION RATES TO BUILD HIS VAST FORTUNE.

GOVERNMENT DECISIONS GAVE MUSK HIS WEALTH AND HE IS USING THAT WEALTH TO SHAPE NOT JUST PUBLIC DISCOURSE BUT THE FUTURE ITSELF DURING A TIME WHEN THE WORLD FACES MULTIPLE CRISES: CLIMATE CHANGE, ENVIRONMENTAL BREAKDOWN, POVERTY, ECONOMIC INEQUALITY, POTENTIAL FURTHER PANDEMICS, AND POTENTIAL NUCLEAR WAR—ANY ONE OF WHICH COULD CAUSE CIVILIZATIONAL COLLAPSE. MUSK'S VIEW APPEARS TO BE THAT HUMANITY'S FUTURE IN SPACE IS MORE IMPORTANT THAN ADDRESSING THE INCREASING ECONOMIC INJUSTICE, RACIAL INEQUALITY, WAR, AND ECOLOGICAL DESTABILIZATION HERE, NOW, ON EARTH.

LONGTERMISM SHAPES MUSK'S THINKING. THIS IS THE WORLDVIEW THAT MANY SILICON VALLEY TECH BILLIONAIRES SUBSCRIBE TO, INCLUDING MUSK'S ONE-TIME PARTNER AT PAYPAL, PETER THIEL. PHILOSOPHER WILLIAM MACASKILL DEFINES LONGTERMISM IN HIS BOOK *WHAT WE OWE THE FUTURE* AS "THE VIEW THAT POSITIVELY INFLUENCING THE LONGTERM FUTURE IS A KEY MORAL PRIORITY OF OUR TIME."
FUTURE

LONGTERMISTS ASK: IF YOU WANT TO DO "THE MOST GOOD," SHOULD YOU FOCUS ON HELPING PEOPLE WHO ARE ALIVE IN THE PRESENT (ROUGHLY EIGHT BILLION PEOPLE) OR THE VAST NUMBERS OF POSSIBLE PEOPLE LIVING IN THE FAR FUTURE?

FROM THIS PERSPECTIVE, THE NEEDS OF A MERE EIGHT BILLION MIGHT BE SEEN AS OUTWEIGHED BY THE NEEDS OF TRILLIONS OF FUTURE PEOPLE. IT'S A LOGIC THAT INEVITABLY LEADS TO AN INDIFFERENCE TO CURRENT GLOBAL ISSUES, EVEN THOUGH MANY OF THESE PROBLEMS HAVE REACHED CRISIS LEVELS.

LONGTERMISM IS A DANGEROUS IDEOLOGY BUILT AROUND THE WORSHIP OF "FUTURE VALUE," WHERE YOU ARE ETHICALLY EXCUSED FROM WORRYING ABOUT THREATS LIKE CLIMATE CHANGE AND GLOBAL POVERTY, BUT BELIEVE YOURSELF TO BE A MORALLY SUPERIOR PERSON FOR FOCUSING INSTEAD ON HUMANITY'S FUTURE.
SUPERIOR MAN
NO ONE SHOULD HAVE THE UNACCOUNTABLE POWER ELON MUSK HAS. HE HAS NOT EARNED IT. HE DID NOT GAIN IT ALONE. DOES HE UNDERSTAND JUST HOW MUCH PRIVILEGE AND LUCK PLAYED IN HIS SUCCESS? HE SEEMS TO BELIEVE HE'S FAR MORE CLEVER THAN HE ACTUALLY IS.

¡VIVA LA LIBERTAD, CARAJO
THE SHADOW PRESIDENT?
Make America Great Again

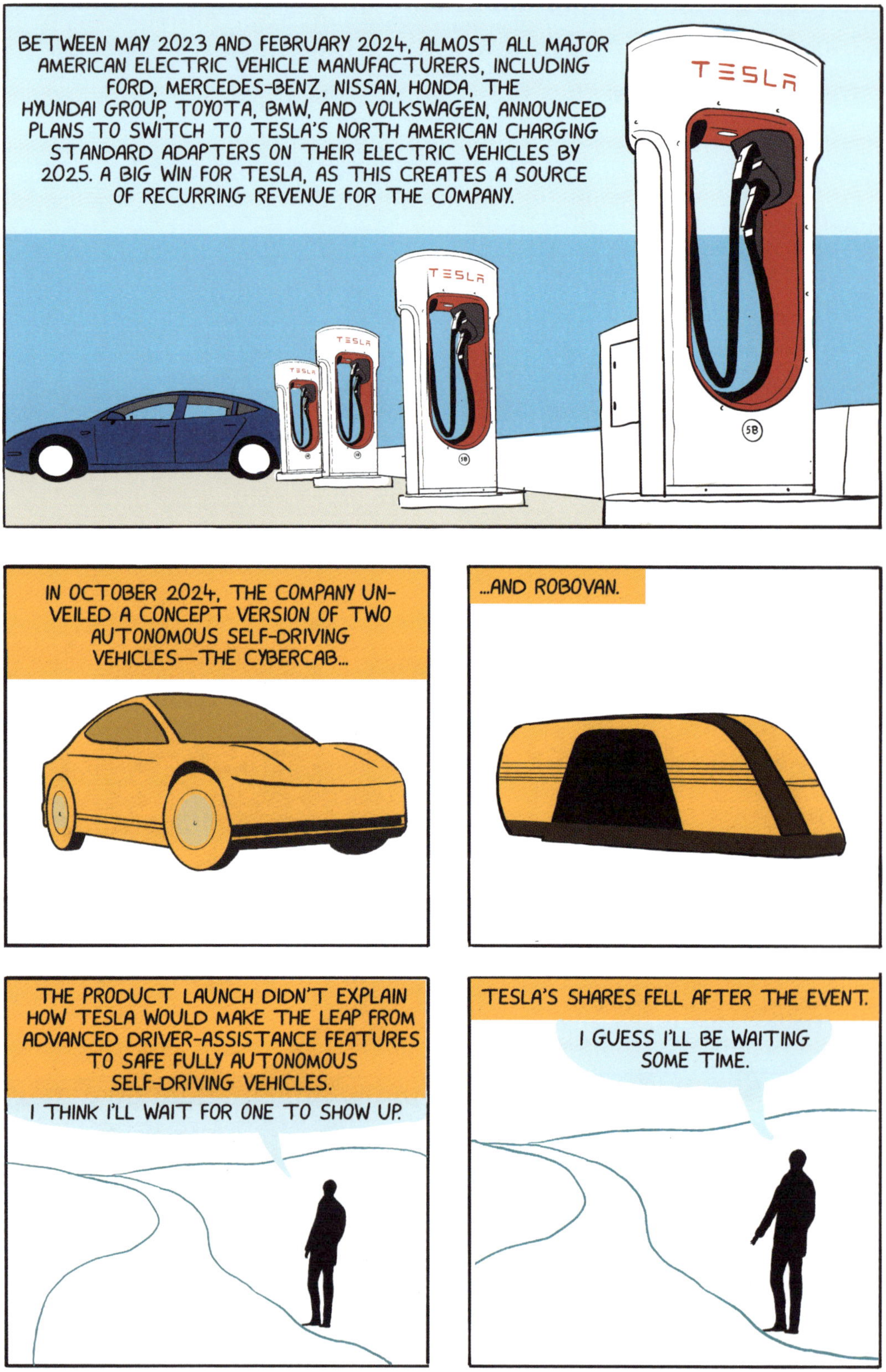

BETWEEN MAY 2023 AND FEBRUARY 2024, ALMOST ALL MAJOR AMERICAN ELECTRIC VEHICLE MANUFACTURERS, INCLUDING FORD, MERCEDES-BENZ, NISSAN, HONDA, THE HYUNDAI GROUP, TOYOTA, BMW, AND VOLKSWAGEN, ANNOUNCED PLANS TO SWITCH TO TESLA'S NORTH AMERICAN CHARGING STANDARD ADAPTERS ON THEIR ELECTRIC VEHICLES BY 2025. A BIG WIN FOR TESLA, AS THIS CREATES A SOURCE OF RECURRING REVENUE FOR THE COMPANY.
TESLA
IN OCTOBER 2024, THE COMPANY UNVEILED A CONCEPT VERSION OF TWO AUTONOMOUS SELF-DRIVING VEHICLES—THE CYBERCAB...
...AND ROBOVAN.
THE PRODUCT LAUNCH DIDN'T EXPLAIN HOW TESLA WOULD MAKE THE LEAP FROM ADVANCED DRIVER-ASSISTANCE FEATURES TO SAFE FULLY AUTONOMOUS SELF-DRIVING VEHICLES.
I THINK I'LL WAIT FOR ONE TO SHOW UP.
TESLA'S SHARES FELL AFTER THE EVENT.
I GUESS I'LL BE WAITING SOME TIME.

ON JANUARY 1, 2025, A TESLA CYBERTRUCK EXPLODED OUTSIDE THE MAIN ENTRANCE OF THE TRUMP INTERNATIONAL HOTEL LAS VEGAS, LOCATED IN PARADISE, NEVADA. THE VEHICLE'S OCCUPANT DIED FROM A SELF-INFLICTED GUNSHOT WOUND TO THE HEAD IMMEDIATELY BEFORE THE EXPLOSION. SEVEN BYSTANDERS WERE INJURED. THE VEHICLE CONTAINED FIREWORK MORTARS AND GAS CANISTERS, WHICH FUELED THE EXPLOSION AND FIRE.
TRUMP
AUTHORITIES IDENTIFIED THE DRIVER AS MATTHEW ALAN LIVELSBERGER, AN AMERICAN-BORN, ACTIVE-DUTY UNITED STATES ARMY SPECIAL FORCES SOLDIER FROM COLORADO SPRINGS, COLORADO, WHO WAS ON LEAVE FROM OVERSEAS DUTY.
LIVELSBERGER'S MOTIVE REMAINS CONTRADICTORY. IN NOTES RECOVERED BY INVESTIGATORS HE WROTE THAT THE INCIDENT WAS INTENDED NOT AS A "TERRORIST ATTACK?" BUT RATHER "A WAKE UP CALL."
HE SAID THE US WAS "TERMINALLY ILL" AND HEADED TOWARDS COLLAPSE. HE ALSO EXPRESSED SUPPORT FOR DONALD TRUMP AND ELON MUSK.
THIS EVENT, TYING TOGETHER AS IT DOES, TRUMP, MUSK, AND WHITE MALE RIGHT-WING RAGE, SEEMED TO FORESHADOW THE SECOND TRUMP ADMINISTRATION, A DARKER ERA IN WHICH ELON MUSK WOULD PLAY A PROMINENT PART.

SIX WEEKS EARLIER, THE SIXTH STARSHIP TEST FLIGHT HAD TAKEN PLACE. BLASTING OFF FROM BOCA CHICA, TEXAS, WITH DONALD TRUMP AMONG THE DIGNITARIES WATCHING.
AFTER DISENGAGING FROM THE STARSHIP...
...THE PLAN WAS FOR THE SUPER HEAVY BOOSTER ROCKET TO RETURN TO ITS LAUNCH PAD FOR CAPTURE BY A GIANT SET OF MECHANICAL ARMS.
THIS AMAZING FEAT HAD BEEN ACHIEVED DURING THE PREVIOUS TEST FLIGHT IN OCTOBER 2024, BUT THIS TIME THE ATTEMPT WAS CALLED OFF DUE TO TECHNICAL DIFFICULTIES. INSTEAD, THE BOOSTER MADE SPLASHDOWN IN THE GULF OF MEXICO.
MEANWHILE THE STARSHIP ENTERED ITS COAST PHASE, FLYING ON THROUGH THE NIGHT.
AFTER THE SHIP SUCCESSFULLY DEMONSTRATED THE PROPULSION SYSTEM'S ABILITY TO PERFORM CRITICAL MANEUVERS IN SPACE, IT MADE REENTRY AND SPLASHED DOWN IN THE INDIAN OCEAN.

BACK IN JULY 2022, AFTER MUSK STATED THAT TRUMP WAS TOO OLD TO HAVE A SECOND TERM AS US PRESIDENT, TRUMP RESPONDED BY WRITING ON TRUTH SOCIAL...
WHEN ELON MUSK CAME TO THE WHITE HOUSE ASKING ME FOR HELP ON ALL OF HIS MANY SUBSIDIZED PROJECTS, WHETHER IT'S ELECTRIC CARS THAT DON'T DRIVE LONG ENOUGH...
...DRIVERLESS CARS THAT CRASH, OR ROCKET-SHIPS TO NOWHERE, WITHOUT WHICH SUBSIDIES HE'D BE WORTHLESS, AND TELL ME HOW HE WAS A BIG TRUMP FAN AND A REPUBLICAN...
...I COULD HAVE SAID, "DROP TO YOUR KNEES AND BEG," AND HE WOULD HAVE DONE IT.
BY THE TIME OF THE 2024 US PRESIDENTIAL ELECTION THE ACRIMONIOUS RELATIONSHIP BETWEEN THE TWO MEN HAD DRAMATICALLY REVERSED.
AS WE HAVE SEEN WITH CHINA AND TURKEY, MUSK WILL HAPPILY BE SUBSERVIENT TO AUTHORITARIANS IF IT HELPS ADVANCE HIS INTERESTS.

THIS DISPLAY OF SERVITUDE ISN'T JUST TO PROMOTE BUSINESS. MUSK HAS A POLITICAL AND CULTURAL VISION THAT ALIGNS CLOSELY WITH THAT OF THE MAGA RIGHT.
SHRINK GOVERNMENT, DECREASE REGULATION, AND END THE WOKE MIND VIRUS
I'M NOT JUST MAGA. I'M DARK GOTHIC MAGA.
MAKE AMERICA GREAT AGAIN
FEDERAL ELECTION COMMISSION FILINGS SHOW THAT ELON MUSK SPENT MORE THAN A QUARTER OF A BILLION DOLLARS TO BACK DONALD TRUMP AND OTHER MAGA CANDIDATES IN THE 2024 US ELECTION.

WHAT DID MUSK GET IN RETURN FOR HIS ENORMOUS "INVESTMENT"? AFTER WINNING THE ELECTION, TRUMP CHOSE MUSK TO LEAD THE NEWLY-FORMED DEPARTMENT OF GOVERNMENT EFFICIENCY (DOGE), WHICH IS TASKED WITH SLASHING GOVERNMENT SPENDING.
VIVA LA LIBERTAD, CARAJO
CHAINSAW GIVEN TO MUSK BY ARGENTINA'S LIBERTARIAN PRESIDENT JAVIER MILEI, ENGRAVED WITH THE SLOGAN "VIVA LA LIBERTAD, CARAJO," WHICH LOOSELY TRANSLATES TO "LONG LIVE FREEDOM, DAMN IT!"

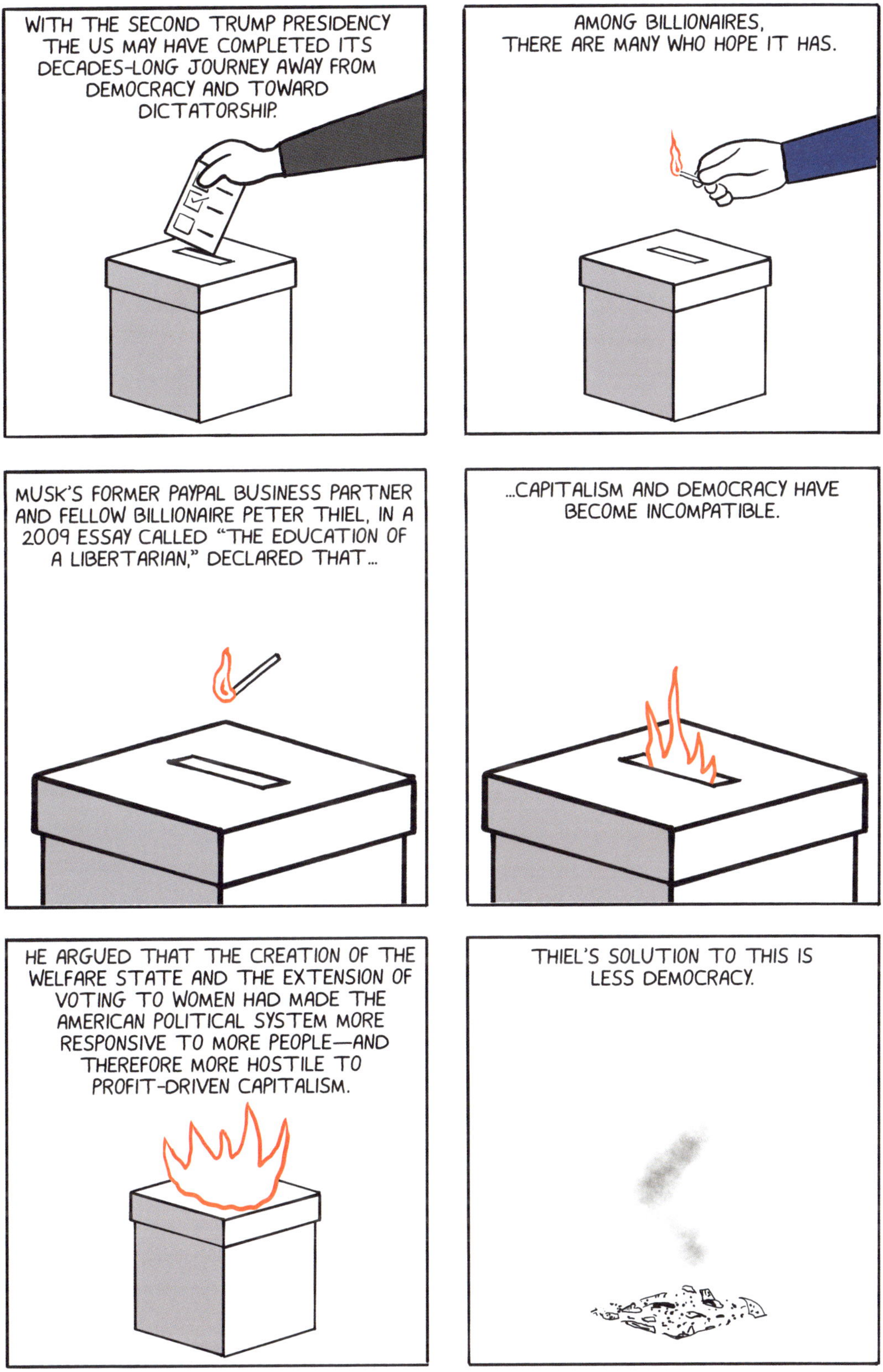
WITH THE SECOND TRUMP PRESIDENCY THE US MAY HAVE COMPLETED ITS DECADES-LONG JOURNEY AWAY FROM DEMOCRACY AND TOWARD DICTATORSHIP.
AMONG BILLIONAIRES, THERE ARE MANY WHO HOPE IT HAS.
MUSK'S FORMER PAYPAL BUSINESS PARTNER AND FELLOW BILLIONAIRE PETER THIEL, IN A 2009 ESSAY CALLED "THE EDUCATION OF A LIBERTARIAN," DECLARED THAT...
...CAPITALISM AND DEMOCRACY HAVE BECOME INCOMPATIBLE.
HE ARGUED THAT THE CREATION OF THE WELFARE STATE AND THE EXTENSION OF VOTING TO WOMEN HAD MADE THE AMERICAN POLITICAL SYSTEM MORE RESPONSIVE TO MORE PEOPLE—AND THEREFORE MORE HOSTILE TO PROFIT-DRIVEN CAPITALISM.
THIEL'S SOLUTION TO THIS IS LESS DEMOCRACY.

I NO LONGER BELIEVE THAT FREEDOM AND DEMOCRACY ARE COMPATIBLE.
PETER THIEL.
FREEDOM FOR BILLIONAIRE BUSINESSMEN APPEARS TO MEAN FREEDOM TO EXPLOIT WORKERS, POLLUTE THE ENVIRONMENT, CREATE MONOPOLIES, PAY NO TAXES, AND BREAK THE LAW WITHOUT CONSEQUENCES.
RU LES
DOES MUSK HOLD THE SAME BELIEFS AS THIEL? SPENDING MILLIONS TO ELECT MAGA POLITICIANS AND USING TWITTER TO DISPARAGE RIVALS AND PROMOTE RADICAL RIGHT-WING IDEOLOGY SUGGESTS HE DOES.
A SOUTH AFRICAN CHILDHOOD IS SOMETHING THIEL SHARES WITH MUSK. THIEL SPENT YEARS OF HIS CHILDHOOD IN SOUTH AFRICA AND NAMIBIA, WHERE HIS FATHER WAS INVOLVED IN URANIUM MINING FOR THE APARTHEID REGIME.
AS ABHORRENT AS IT MAY SEEM, APARTHEID SOUTH AFRICA MAY BE THE MODEL OF WHAT MUSK, THIEL, AND MANY OTHER BILLIONAIRES ENVISION AS THE FUTURE OF THE UNITED STATES.
A BRUTALLY UNEQUAL, MISOGYNISTIC, RACIST SOCIETY, IN WHICH THE POOR AND SHRINKING MIDDLE CLASS SERVES THE INTERESTS OF THE NEVER-TAXED AND MOSTLY WHITE SUPER RICH.

HAS MUSK BEEN A POSITIVE FORCE FOR HUMANITY? TESLA HAS HELPED PUSH FORWARD THE WIDESPREAD INTRODUCTION OF ELECTRIC VEHICLES AND SPACEX HAS BROUGHT DOWN THE COSTS OF THE SPACE INDUSTRY. BUT ANY GOOD MUSK HAS DONE FOR THE WORLD HAS BEEN EXTINGUISHED BY HIS EFFORTS TO BRING TO POWER AN AUTOCRATIC AND REPRESSIVE REGIME IN THE UNITED STATES.
FROM 2024 ONWARDS, MUSK BEGAN EXTENDING HIS POLITICAL INFLUENCE BEYOND THE US THROUGH AN ESCALATING SERIES OF ATTACKS ON EUROPEAN LEADERS AND GOVERNMENTS.
MUSK CRITICIZED THE BRITISH PRIME MINISTER KEIR STARMER AMID A DOMESTIC DEBATE IN THE UK ABOUT HISTORIC CASES OF THE SEXUAL GROOMING OF CHILDREN BY GANGS OF BRITISH MEN WHO WERE MAINLY OF PAKISTANI DESCENT.
THE FAR RIGHT IN THE UK HAS USED THIS ISSUE TO ATTACK IMMIGRANT COMMUNITIES WHILE BEING SILENT ABOUT WHITE MEN WHO COMMIT THE SAME OFFENSE.
ENGLISH DEFENCE LEAGUE
RAPE MURDER HATRED
For Gods Sake Do Something
MUSK TWEETED THAT KING CHARLES SHOULD DISSOLVE PARLIAMENT AND THAT STARMER SHOULD BE IN JAIL.
AMERICA SHOULD LIBERATE THE PEOPLE OF BRITAIN FROM THEIR TYRANNICAL GOVERNMENT.

I ENJOY THE CUT AND THRUST OF POLITICS, THE ROBUST DEBATE THAT WE MUST HAVE, BUT THAT'S GOT TO BE BASED ON FACTS AND TRUTH, NOT ON LIES, NOT ON THOSE WHO ARE SO DESPERATE FOR ATTENTION THAT THEY'RE PREPARED TO DEBASE THEMSELVES.
SIR KEIR STARMER.
IN DECEMBER 2024, MUSK WROTE THAT "ONLY THE AFD CAN SAVE GERMANY," REFERRING TO THE ALTERNATIVE FOR GERMANY, A RIGHT-WING POPULIST POLITICAL PARTY THAT OPPOSES IMMIGRATION, ESPECIALLY MUSLIM IMMIGRATION.
AfD
BACK IN MAY, BJÖRN HÖCKE, THE LEADER OF THE AFD IN THE EASTERN REGION OF THURINGIA, WAS CONVICTED OF USING A SLOGAN ASSOCIATED WITH THE NAZI PARTY'S PARAMILITARY WING, THE STURMABTEILUNG, IN A SPEECH AT A 2021 CAMPAIGN EVENT.
EVERYTHING FOR GERMANY.
DURING A LIVESTREAMED DISCUSSION BROADCAST ON X WITH ALICE WEIDEL, LEADER OF THE AFD, ON JANUARY 9, 2025, MUSK SAID...
PEOPLE REALLY NEED TO GET BEHIND AFD, OTHERWISE THINGS ARE GOING TO GET VERY, VERY MUCH WORSE IN GERMANY.
TEN YEARS AGO, WHO WOULD HAVE IMAGINED THAT THE OWNER OF ONE OF THE LARGEST SOCIAL NETWORKS WOULD BE SUPPORTING A NEW INTERNATIONAL REACTIONARY MOVEMENT AND INTERVENING DIRECTLY IN ELECTIONS?
FRENCH PRESIDENT EMMANUEL MACRON.
(MUSK) ATTACKS OUR INSTITUTIONS, STIRS UP HATRED, AND OPENLY CALLS FOR THE SUPPORT OF THE HEIRS OF NAZISM IN GERMANY'S UPCOMING ELECTIONS.
SPANISH PRIME MINISTER PEDRO SÁNCHEZ.

THE JOURNEY ELON MUSK HAS MADE FROM BULLIED NERD TO TECH TYCOON HAS BEEN A LONG ONE. IT'S OFTEN BEEN DIFFICULT TO SEE WHO HE IS, BUT ON JANUARY 20, 2025, ELON MUSK MADE TWO GESTURES THAT LOOKED TO MANY OBSERVERS LIKE NAZI SALUTES DURING HIS SPEECH AT PRESIDENT DONALD TRUMP'S INAUGURATION. MUSK DENIED THE GESTURES WERE SALUTES. YET TAKEN WITH OTHER EVIDENCE, THESE GESTURES SHOW QUITE CLEARLY WHO ELON MUSK IS, AND WHAT HIS AIMS ARE. WE SHOULD NOW DISPENSE WITH THE ILLUSION THAT HE CARES FOR DEMOCRACY, FREE SPEECH, OR THE WELL-BEING OF HUMANITY. HIS ADVOCACY OF FAR-RIGHT POLITICAL MOVEMENTS, HIS ABILITY TO SHAPE PUBLIC OPINION, AND HIS PARTNERSHIP WITH DONALD TRUMP, MAKE IT CLEAR THAT HE'S A SERIOUS DANGER TO DEMOCRACY EVERYWHERE.

THE SIMILARITIES BETWEEN MUSK'S TECH-AUTHORITARIANISM AND HIS GRANDFATHER JOSHUA NORMAN HALDEMAN'S BELIEF IN TECHNOCRACY ARE OBVIOUS. MUSK PROMOTES MANY OF THE SAME VALUES, WHICH ARE: RULE BY A TECHNOCRAT ELITE, AND FREEDOM FROM DEMOCRACY. IT IS AN UGLY VISION AND ONE THE WORLD SHOULD REJECT.

ACKNOWLEDGMENTS

As always with my nonfiction books I didn't write this alone. I'm indebted to the innumerable journalists whose work I've drawn from to create this book. I'm particularly indebted to the following writers and their books: *A Woman Makes a Plan: Advice for a Lifetime of Adventure, Beauty and Success* by Maye Musk, *Ludicrous: The Unvarnished Story of Tesla Motors* by Edward Niedermeyer, *Elon Musk: Tesla, SpaceX, and the Quest for a Fantastic Future* by Ashlee Vance, *The Space Barons: Elon Musk, Jeff Bezos, and the Quest to Colonize the Cosmos* by Christian Davenport, *Power Play: Tesla, Elon Musk, and the Bet of the Century* by Tim Higgins, *The Founders: The Story of PayPal and the Entrepreneurs Who Shaped Silicon Valley* by Jimmy Soni, and *Elon Musk* by Walter Isaacson. All are essential reading if you want to explore the various subjects of this book in more detail.

Thanks are also due to Simon Fraser, Nick Abadzis, Nichola Taylor, Daniel Isca, Nicolas Grivel, and all at Seven Stories Press.

And most of all to Bonnie Millard for her constant and unwavering love and support.

REFERENCES

BOOKS

Davenport, Christian. 2018. *The Space Barons: Elon Musk, Jeff Bezos, and the Quest to Colonize the Cosmos*. New York: PublicAffairs.

Higgins, Tim. 2021. *Power Play: Tesla, Elon Musk, and the Bet of the Century*. New York: Doubleday.

Isaacson, Walter. 2023. *Elon Musk*. New York: Simon & Schuster.

Musk, Maye. 2019. *A Woman Makes a Plan: Advice for a Lifetime of Adventure, Beauty, and Success*. New York: Viking Life.

Niedermeyer, Edward. 2019. *Ludicrous: The Unvarnished Story of Tesla Motors*. Dallas: BenBella Books.

Soni, Jimmy. 2022. *The Founders: The Story of PayPal and the Entrepreneurs Who Shaped Silicon Valley*. New York: Simon & Schuster.

Vance, Ashlee. 2015. *Elon Musk: Tesla, SpaceX, and the Quest for a Fantastic Future*. London: Virgin Books.

ONLINE ARTICLES

Early Life and Family

Argyle, Ray. "The Last Utopians. Technocracy Promised Depression-Weary Canadians an End to Their Hardship. But the Offer Came with a Catch." *Canada's History*, January 1, 2018. https://www.canadashistory.ca/explore/politics-law/the-last-utopians.

Baker, Sinéad, Grace Kay, and Phillip de Wet. "Elon Musk's Parents: Errol and Maye Musk, the Figures Behind the Tesla CEO's Success." *Business Insider*, July 17, 2023. https://www.businessinsider.com/elon-musk-parents.

Canada: A People's History. "Social Credit Party. William 'Bible Bill' Aberhart Combines Salvation with Economics—and a New Political Party Is Born." CBC, n.d. https://www.cbc.ca/history/EPISCONTENTSE1EP13CH3PA2LE.html.

Haldeman, Scott, and Joseph C. Keating, Jr. "Joshua N. Haldeman, DC: The Canadian Years, 1926–1950." *The Journal of the Canadian Chiropractic Association* 39, no. 3 (1995): 163–178. https://www.ncbi.nlm.nih.gov/pmc/articles/PMC2485067.

Harrison, Ellie, and Charlotte Cripps. "Talulah Riley Says She 'Understands It Looks Strange' That She Married Elon Musk Twice." *The Independent*, July 20, 2022. https://www.independent.co.uk/arts-entertainment/books/news/elon-musk-talulah-riley-relationship-b2114732.html.

Hartmans, Avery. "Elon Musk Says His Teenage Daughter Doesn't Want to Be Associated with Him Because of What He Calls 'Full-On Communism' Taught in Schools and Widespread Hatred of the Wealthy." *Business Insider*, October 7, 2022. https://www.businessinsider.com/elon-musk-blames-communism-hatred-of-wealthy-for-daughters-estrangement-2022-10.

Hartmans, Avery, Sinéad Baker, Grace Kay, and Kylie Kirschner. "Elon Musk's Famous Family Includes a Movie Producer, Dirt-Bike Rider, and Several Millionaire Cousins." *Business Insider*, September 11, 2023. https://www.businessinsider.com/elon-musk-family-tree.

Mann, Jyoti, and Grace Dean. "Elon Musk Really Was Telling the Truth by Saying His Father Errol Never Owned an Emerald Mine, Biographer Says." *Business Insider*, September 11, 2023. https://www.businessinsider.com/elon-musk-father-errol-never-owned-emerald-mine-telling-truth-2023-9.

Mann, Mark. "The Story of Elon Musk's First Company." *SiteBuilderReport*, June 16, 2022. https://www.sitebuilderreport.com/origin-stories/elon-musk.

Musk, Justine. "'I Was a Starter Wife': Inside America's Messiest Divorce." *Marie Claire*, September 10, 2010. https://www.marieclaire.com/sex-love/a5380/millionaire-starter-wife.

Paul, Kari. "Elon Musk Fathered Twins with One of His Executives Last Year." *The Guardian*, July 6, 2022. https://www.theguardian.com/technology/2022/jul/06/elon-musk-twins-children-shivon-zilis.

Paul, Kari, and agencies. "Elon Musk's Daughter Legally Changes Name and Cuts Ties with Her Father." *The Guardian*, June 21, 2022. https://www.theguardian.com/technology/2022/jun/21/elon-musk-daughter-legal-name-change.

Tesla

Auchard, Eric, and Tova Cohen. "Mobileye Says Tesla Was 'Pushing the Envelope in Terms of Safety'." *Reuters*, September 14, 2016. https://www.reuters.com/article/us-mobileye-tesla-idUSKCN11K2T8.

Auchard, Eric. "Mobileye Says It Warned Tesla Against Enabling 'Hands-Free' Driving." *Reuters*, September 16, 2016. https://www.reuters.com/article/us-mobileye-tesla-idUSKCN11M2GO.

Bruce, Chris. "Tesla Sues Model X Falcon Wing Door Supplier." *Autoblog*, January 25, 2016. https://www.autoblog.com/2016/01/25/tesla-model-x-falcon-wing-supplier-lawsuit.

Burns, Matt. "'Anyone Relying on Lidar Is Doomed,' Elon Musk Says." *TechCrunch*, April 22, 2019. https://techcrunch.com/2019/04/22/anyone-relying-on-lidar-is-doomed-elon-musk-says.

Etherington, Darrell. "NTSB Says Fatal Tesla Autopilot Crash Caused in Part by Resulting Inattention." *TechCrunch*, September 12, 2017. https://techcrunch.com/2017/09/12/ntsb-says-fatal-tesla-autopilot-crash-caused-in-part-by-resulting-inattention.

Hamilton, Isobel Asher. "Tesla 'Whistleblower' Says Elon Musk Is Waging War on Him for Leaking Information to Business Insider." *Business Insider*, June 22, 2018. https://www.businessinsider.com/tesla-whistleblower-martin-tripp-elon-musk-waging-war-on-him-over-leaks-2018-6.

Hawkins, Andrew J. "Tesla Whistleblower Martin Tripp Ordered to Pay $400,000 to Settle Hacking Case." *The Verge*, December 1, 2020. https://www.theverge.com/2020/12/1/21755428/tesla-martin-tripp-settlement-whistleblower-hacing-amount.

Hern, Alex. "Twitter and Tesla's Interests at Odds in Elon Musk's Quiet China Visit." *The Guardian*, June 1, 2023. https://www.theguardian.com/technology/2023/jun/01/elon-musk-china-visit-twitter-tesla.

Klein, Alice. "Tesla Driver Dies in First Fatal Autonomous Car Crash in US." *New Scientist*, July 1, 2016. https://www.newscientist.com/article/2095740-tesla-driver-dies-in-first-fatal-autonomous-car-crash-in-us.

Kolodny, Lora, and Erin Black. "Tesla Founders Martin Eberhard and Marc Tarpenning Talk About the Early Days and Bringing On Elon Musk." *CNBC*, February 6, 2021. https://www.cnbc.com/2021/02/06/tesla-founders-martin-eberhard-marc-tarpenning-on-elon-musk.html.

Krizek, Kevin J. "Ever-Larger Cars and Trucks Are Causing a Safety Crisis on US Streets. Here's How Communities Can Fight Back." *The Conversation*, August 2, 2023. https://theconversation.com/ever-larger-cars-and-trucks-are-causing-a-safety-crisis-on-us-streets-heres-how-communities-can-fight-back-206382.

Lee, Timothy B. "In 2017, the Feds Said Tesla Autopilot Cut Crashes 40%. That Was Bogus." *ArsTechnica*, February 13, 2019. https://arstechnica.com/cars/2019/02/in-2017-the-feds-said-tesla-autopilot-cut-crashes-40-that-was-bogus.

Lopez, Linette. "The Bizarre Case of Elon Musk and the Tesla Whistleblower Has Closed, but Questions About Millions of Dollars Wasted at the Gigafactory Remain." *Business Insider*, December 1, 2020. https://www.businessinsider.com/tesla-millions-dollars-waste-gigafactory-martin-tripp-court-documents-2020-12.

Marshall, Aarian. "Tesla Bears Some Blame for Self-Driving Crash Death, Feds Say." *Wired*, September 13, 2017. https://www.wired.com/story/tesla-ntsb-autopilot-crash-death.

Niedermeyer, Edward. "When I First Saw Elon Musk for Who He Really Is." *Slate*, May 27, 2022. https://slate.com/technology/2022/05/elon-musk-tesla-twitter-fables.html.

Ohnsman, Alan. "The Business Case for Musk's Tesla Cybertruck Isn't Bulletproof." *Forbes*, December 8, 2023. https://www.forbes.com/sites/alanohnsman/2023/12/08/the-business-case-for-musks-tesla-cybertruck-isnt-bulletproof.

Reuters. "Transport Safety Body Rules Safeguards 'Were Lacking' in Deadly Tesla Crash." *The Guardian*, September 12, 2017. https://www.theguardian.com/technology/2017/sep/12/tesla-crash-joshua-brown-safety-self-driving-cars.

Reuters. "Tesla Stops Taking Orders for Cybertruck Outside North America." *CNBC*, May 17, 2022. https://www.cnbc.com/2022/05/17/tesla-stops-taking-orders-for-cybertruck-outside-north-america.html.

Robinson, Matt, and Zeke Faux. "When Elon Musk Tried to Destroy a Tesla Whistleblower." *Bloomberg*, March 13, 2019. https://www.bloomberg.com/news/features/2019-03-13/when-elon-musk-tried-to-destroy-tesla-whistleblower-martin-tripp.

Sriram, Akash, and Hyunjoo Jin. "Tesla Cybertruck's Stiff Structure, Sharp Design Raise Safety Concerns." *Reuters*, December 8, 2023. https://www.reuters.com/business/autos-transportation/tesla-cybertrucks-stiff-structure-sharp-design-raise-safety-concerns-experts-2023-12-08.

Stevens, Tim. "Mobileye CEO: Tesla Accepting Higher Risk to Lower Its Autonomy Costs." *CNET*, May 21, 2018. https://www.cnet.com/roadshow/news/mobileye-ceo-tesla-self-driving-cars.

"Tesla: A History of Innovation (and Headaches)." *Forbes*, September 29, 2022. https://www.forbes.com/sites/qai/2022/09/29/tesla-a-history-of-innovation-and-headaches.

"What Is LiDAR and How Does It Work?" *Geoslam*. https://geoslam.com/what-is-lidar.

"What is ZEV?" *Union of Concerned Scientists*, August 7, 2012. https://www.ucsusa.org/resources/what-zev.

SpaceX and Starlink

Associated Press, "SpaceX Rocket Failure Traced to Bad Nut." *NBC News*, July 19, 2006. https://www.nbcnews.com/id/wbna13933540.

Bartels, Megan. "SpaceX's Starship Fails Upward in Milestone Test." *Scientific American*, April 20, 2023. https://www.scientificamerican.com/article/spacex-powerful-starship-explodes-after-launch.

Crist, Ry, and Trey Paul. "Starlink Explained: What You Need to Know About Elon Musk's Satellite Internet Service." *CNET*, June 20, 2023. https://www.cnet.com/home/internet/starlink-satellite-internet-explained.

Fortner, Robert. "Sustainable Rocketry: SpaceX to Cut Launch Costs with Reusable Rocket." *ArsTechnica*, October 2011. https://arstechnica.com/science/2011/10/sustainable-rocketry-spacex-to-cut-launch-costs-with-reusable-rocket.

Hennigan, W.J. "SpaceX Says It's Developing the First Fully Reusable Rocket." *Los Angeles Times*, September 29, 2011. https://www.latimes.com/archives/blogs/money-company/story/2011-09-29/spacex-says-its-developing-the-first-fully-reusable-rocket.

Kang, Cecilia, and Christian Davenport. "SpaceX Founder Files with Government to Provide Internet Service from Space." *Washington Post*, June 9, 2015. https://www.washingtonpost.com/business/economy/spacex-founder-files-with-government-to-provide-internet-service-from-space/2015/06/09/db8d8d02-0eb7-11e5-a0dc-2b6f404ff5cf_story.html.

Kolodny, Lora. "SpaceX Starship Explosion Spread Particulate Matter for Miles." *CNBC*, April 24, 2023. https://www.cnbc.com/2023/04/24/spacex-starship-explosion-spread-particulate-matter-for-miles.html.

Mallama, Anthony. "Starlink Satellites Are Fainter Now, but Still Visible." *Sky and Telescope*, January 22, 2021. https://skyandtelescope.org/astronomy-news/starlink-satellites-fainter-but-still-visible.

Mazurenko, Alona. "First Surface Vessel Attack on Crimea Failed as Musk Turned Off Connection." *Ukrainska Pravda*, January 1, 2024. https://www.pravda.com.ua/eng/news/2024/01/1/7435389.

Miller, Andrea. "Design Error May Have Caused SpaceX Rocket Explosion in 2015: NASA." *ABC News*, March 13, 2018. https://abcnews.go.com/Technology/design-error-caused-spacex-rocket-explosion-2015-nasa/story?id=53710225.

Wagstaff, Keith, and Devin Coldewey. "SpaceX Makes History: Falcon 9 Launches, Lands Vertically." *NBC News*, December 21, 2015. https://www.nbcnews.com/tech/innovation/spacex-makes-history-successfully-launches-lands-falcon-9-rocket-n483921.

Young, Chris. "Watch SpaceX Spray Thousands of Gallons of Water for Starship Test." *Interesting Engineering*, July 19, 2023. https://interestingengineering.com/innovation/watch-spacex-spray-thousands-gallons-of-water-starship-test.

Twitter

Conger, Kate, Mike Isaac, Ryan Mac, and Tiffany Hsu. "Two Weeks of Chaos: Inside Elon Musk's Takeover of Twitter." *New York Times*, November 11, 2022. https://www.nytimes.com/2022/11/11/technology/elon-musk-twitter-takeover.html.

Gault, Matthew. "Free Speech Warrior Elon Musk Weaker on Government Censorship Than the Twitter Execs He Fired." *Vice*, May 17, 2023. https://www.vice.com/en/article/88xqnv/elon-musk-censors-twitter-in-turkey.

Jin, Hyunjoo, and Chibuike Oguh. "Explainer: How Elon Musk Funded the $44 Billion Twitter Deal." *Reuters*, October 28, 2022. https://www.reuters.com/markets/us/how-will-elon-musk-pay-twitter-2022-10-07.

Milmo, Dan. "Elon Musk Fires Additional 200 People at Twitter, Report Says." *The Guardian*, February 27, 2023. https://www.theguardian.com/technology/2023/feb/27/elon-musk-fires-additional-200-people-at-twitter-report-says.

Other

Artsy, Avishay. "Elon Musk's Tunnels to Nowhere." *Vox*, December 8, 2022. https://www.vox.com/recode/2022/12/8/23498861/elon-musk-boring-company-tunnels-finished.

Brandom, Russell. "Elon Musk Reveals Plans for High-Speed Hyperloop." *The Verge*, August 12, 2013. https://www.theverge.com/2013/8/12/4614940/elon-musk-reveals-plans-for-high-speed-hyperloop.

Conger, Kate, Mike Isaac, Ryan Mac, and Tiffany Hsu. "Two Weeks of Chaos: Inside Elon Musk's Takeover of Twitter." *New York Times*, November 11, 2022. https://www.nytimes.com/2022/11/11/technology/elon-musk-twitter-takeover.html.

Dawkins, David. “Elon Musk Brands Himself an ‘Idiot’ in Thai Cave Rescue Defamation Lawsuit.” *Forbes*, October 9, 2019. https://www.forbes.com/sites/daviddawkins/2019/10/09/elon-musk-brands-himself-an-idiot-in-thai-cave-rescue-defamation-lawsuit.

Dodds, Io. “From Self-Proclaimed ‘Socialist’ to Team Trump and DeSantis: Elon Musk’s Curious Politics Revealed.” *The Independent*, May 24, 2023. https://www.independent.co.uk/news/world/americas/us-politics/elon-musk-twitter-deal-politics-b2345301.html.

Folk, Zachary. “Elon Musk Claims ‘Not Even Trace Amounts’ of Drugs in His System After Report Detailed Drug Concerns from Tesla, SpaceX Execs.” *Forbes*, January 7, 2024. https://www.forbes.com/sites/zacharyfolk/2024/01/07/elon-musk-claims-not-even-trace-amounts-of-drugs-in-his-system-after-report-detailed-drug-concerns-from-tesla-spacex-execs.

Gault, Matthew. “Free Speech Warrior Elon Musk Weaker on Government Censorship Than the Twitter Execs He Fired.” *Vice*, May 17, 2023. https://www.vice.com/en/article/88xqnv/elon-musk-censors-twitter-in-turkey.

Glazer, Emily, and Kirsten Grind. “Elon Musk Has Used Illegal Drugs, Worrying Leaders at Tesla and SpaceX.” *Wall Street Journal*, January 6, 2024. https://www.wsj.com/business/elon-musk-illegal-drugs-e826a9e1.

Jin, Hyunjoo, and Chibuike Oguh. “Explainer: How Elon Musk Funded the $44 Billion Twitter Deal.” *Reuters*, October 28, 2022. https://www.reuters.com/markets/us/how-will-elon-musk-pay-twitter-2022-10-07.

Kolodny, Lora. “Elon Musk’s Neuralink Hype Irks Rivals Yet Shines a Light on Brain Implants.” *Financial Times*, February 3, 2024. https://www.ft.com/content/da52aa61-4b9a-435a-aa5c-eaf4c6e01dcb.

Kolodny, Lora. “Elon Musk Found Not Liable in ‘Pedo Guy’ Defamation Trial.” *CNBC*, December 6, 2019. https://www.cnbc.com/2019/12/06/unsworth-vs-musk-pedo-guy-defamation-trial-verdict.html.

Lalljee, Jason. “Elon Musk Is Speaking Out Against Government Subsidies. Here’s a List of the Billions of Dollars His Businesses Have Received.” *Business Insider*, December 15, 2021. https://www.businessinsider.com/elon-musk-list-government-subsidies-tesla-billions-spacex-solarcity-2021-12.

Levin, Sam. “Elon Musk Calls British Diver in Thai Cave Rescue ‘Pedo’ in Baseless Attack.” *The Guardian*, July 16, 2018. https://www.theguardian.com/technology/2018/jul/15/elon-musk-british-diver-thai-cave-rescue-pedo-twitter.

Levitz, Eric. "Elon Musk's Politics Are About as Complicated as Trump's." *New York Magazine*, December 14, 2022. https://nymag.com/intelligencer/2022/12/is-elon-musk-conservative-donald-trump.html.

Levy, Rachael. "Musk's Neuralink Faces Federal Probe, Employee Backlash over Animal Tests." *Reuters*, December 6, 2022. https://www.reuters.com/technology/musks-neuralink-faces-federal-probe-employee-backlash-over-animal-tests-2022-12-05.

Levy, Rachael. "Musk Approaches Brain Chip Startup Synchron About Deal amid Neuralink Delays." *Reuters*, August 19, 2022. https://www.reuters.com/technology/musk-approaches-brain-chip-startup-synchron-about-deal-amid-neuralink-delays-2022-08-19.

Pohl, Reina. "Ahead of Elon Musk's 'Show and Tell,' Doctors Group Reveals Disturbing Truth Behind Neuralink Monkey Experiments." *BusinessWire*, November 28, 2022. https://www.businesswire.com/news/home/20221128005672/en/Ahead-of-Elon-Musk's-"Show-and-Tell"-Doctors-Group-Reveals-Disturbing-Truth-Behind-Neuralink-Monkey-Experiments.

Teh, Cheryl. "Elon Musk Says Democrats Have 'Become the Party of Division and Hate,' Repeats Claim That He'll Now Vote Republican." *Business Insider*, May 18, 2022. https://www.businessinsider.com/elon-musk-calls-democrats-party-of-division-and-hate-2022-5.

Warzel, Charlie. "Elon Musk Is a Far-Right Activist." *The Atlantic*, December 11, 2022. https://www.theatlantic.com/technology/archive/2022/12/elon-musk-twitter-far-right-activist/672436.

Waters, Richard, and Michael Peel. "Elon Musk's Neuralink Hype Irks Rivals Yet Shines a Light on Brain Implants." *Financial Times*, February 3, 2024. https://www.ft.com/content/da52aa61-4b9a-435a-aa5c-eaf4c6e01dcb.

"Wealth of Five Richest Men Doubles Since 2020 as Five Billion People Made Poorer in 'Decade of Division,' Says Oxfam." Oxfam Press Release, January 15, 2024. https://www.oxfam.org/en/press-releases/wealth-five-richest-men-doubles-2020-five-billion-people-made-poorer-decade-division.

Whitefoot, John. "Companies That Died and Survived The Dotcom Bubble." *Lombardi Letter*, March 22, 2017. https://www.lombardiletter.com/companies-that-died-and-survived-the-dotcom-bubble/9106.

Wong, Julia Carrie. "Elon Musk Calls British Diver in Thai Cave Rescue 'Pedo' in Baseless Attack." *The Guardian*, July 16, 2018. https://www.theguardian.com/technology/2018/jul/15/elon-musk-british-diver-thai-cave-rescue-pedo-twitter.

News references

Bohannon, Molly. "Elon Musk's SpaceX Launches 5th Starship Test—and Catches Booster in Mid-Air." *Forbes*, October 13, 2024. https://www.forbes.com/sites/mollybohannon/2024/10/13/elon-musks-spacex-launches-5th-starship-test-and-catches-booster-in-mid-air.

Burridge, Tom Soufi. "EU Politicians Warn Against Elon Musk's Incursions into European Politics." *ABC News*, January 9, 2025. https://abcnews.go.com/International/eu-politicians-warn-elon-musks-incursions-european-politics/story?id=117460305.

Cole, Deborah. "German Court Fines Senior AfD Politician €13,000 for Using Banned Nazi Phrase." *The Guardian*, May 14, 2024. https://www.theguardian.com/world/article/2024/may/14/german-court-fines-afd-bjorn-hocke-using-banned-nazi-phrase.

Crerar, Pippa, Rajeev Syal, and Aletha Adu. "Starmer Condemns 'Lies and Misinformation' as He Hits Back at Musk." *The Guardian*, January 6, 2025. https://www.theguardian.com/politics/2025/jan/06/starmer-condemns-lies-and-misinformation-as-he-hits-back-at-musk.

Henley, Jon. "Emmanuel Macron Joins Growing Criticism of Elon Musk in Europe." *The Guardian*, January 6, 2025. https://www.theguardian.com/technology/2025/jan/06/emmanuel-macron-joins-growing-criticism-elon-musk-europe.

Henley, Jon. "How Elon Musk Has Meddled in European Affairs." *The Guardian*, January 11, 2025. https://www.theguardian.com/technology/2025/jan/11/how-elon-musk-has-meddled-in-european-affairs.

Honderich, Holly. "What We Know About Musk's Cost-Cutting Mission." *BBC News*, December 5, 2024. https://www.bbc.co.uk/news/articles/c23vkd57471o.

Hull, Dana, Edward Ludlow, and Kara Carlson. "Tesla Shares Sink After Musk's Robotaxi Unveiling Disappoints." *Bloomberg*, October 11, 2024. https://www.bloomberg.com/news/articles/2024-10-11/musk-shows-tesla-cybercab-sees-sub-30-000-cost-and-2026-debut.

Ingram, Julia, and Steve Reilly. "Elon Musk Spends $277 Million to Back Trump and Republican Candidates." *CBS News*, December 6, 2024. https://www.cbsnews.com/news/elon-musk-277-million-trump-republican-candidates-donations.

Kuper, Simon. "Musk, Thiel, and the Shadow of Apartheid South Africa." *Financial Times*, September 19, 2024. https://www.ft.com/content/cfbfa1e8-d8f8-42b9-b74c-dae6cc6185a0.

Luna, Alfons. “Spanish PM Says Musk ‘Stirs Up Hatred’, Warns Against Fascism.” *Barron’s*, January 8, 2025. https://www.barrons.com/news/spanish-pm-says-musk-stirs-up-hatred-warns-against-fascism-10637837.

Marchall, Aarian. “Tesla Wins EV Charging! Now What?” *Wired*, February 13, 2024. https://www.wired.com/story/tesla-wins-ev-charging-now-what.

“Musk Doubles Down on Support for German Far-Right Leader.” *Le Monde*, January 10, 2025. https://www.lemonde.fr/en/europe/article/2025/01/10/musk-doubles-down-on-support-for-german-far-right-leader_6736883_143.html.

Pengelly, Martin. “Elon Musk Appears to Make Back-to-Back Fascist Salutes at Inauguration Rally.” *The Guardian*, January 20, 2025. https://www.theguardian.com/technology/2025/jan/20/trump-elon-musk-salute.

Phillips, Aleks. “Why Is Elon Musk Becoming Donald Trump’s Efficiency Tsar?” *BBC News*, November 13, 2024. https://www.bbc.co.uk/news/articles/cpqd4vw0ejeo.

“Super Heavy Starship Launches on Sixth Test Flight, Skips Tower Catch.” *Spaceflight Now*, November 20, 2024. https://spaceflightnow.com/2024/11/20/super-heavy-starship-launches-on-sixth-test-flight.

“Trump Steps Up Attacks on Musk, Who Said Trump Needs to ‘Sail into the Sunset’.” *Reuters*, July 13, 2022. https://www.reuters.com/world/us/its-time-trump-sail-into-sunset-says-musk-2022-07-12.

Yousif, Nadine. “Suspect in Cybertruck Blast Suffered from PTSD.” *BBC News*, January 3, 2025. https://www.bbc.co.uk/news/articles/cp3z0x6yx67o.

INDEX